NORWYN DENNY

# *Caring*

## THE PASTORAL MINISTRY OF THE CHRISTIAN COMMUNITY

London EPWORTH PRESS

7162 0275 1

*Enquiries should be addressed to*
*The Methodist Publishing House*
*Wellington Road*
*Wimbledon*
*London SW19 8EU*
*Printed in Great Britain by*
*The Garden City Press Limited*
*Letchworth, Hertfordshire SG6 1JS*

# Contents

# Foreword

The main body of this book was produced in the form of lectures at the Notting Hill Ecumenical Centre during the winter of 1974–5. The people attending took part in the dialogue on the subject of Pastoral Theology and Ministry. The content arises out of experience in ministry in Notting Hill and elsewhere. It goes to support the thesis that the best means of both caring and evangelism is the Christian community alive to its whole ministry. If the original lectures were delivered under pressure, the putting together in this form is done under equal pressure, if in another place. It reminds me again that real ministry occurs in the arena of life and not in some secluded or reflective place. It will no doubt be clear that because of the pressures, it could have been much better done.

It is dedicated to those who made it possible, the live Christian community in Notting Hill, who have made all ministry real and vital to me and to many others.

NORWYN DENNY

*Epiphany 1976*

# 1 On Being the Body of Christ in the World

When we first went to Notting Hill we were engaged almost at once with the problems that battered at our doors. People needed accommodation: rooms that were found for them needed cleaning; lavatories, sometimes one for the whole house of twenty people, needed a lot of cleaning. Then there was furniture to move and the family to be settled as best it could in the circumstances. People were out of work and came to us looking for a job, or for letters to take to firms that might supply one. It took a lot of time and physical effort and in some people's minds had little to do with ministry. It was ministry of course in the basic sense of doing a serving job for people. The social projects that arose because of the needs that were so obvious, went hand in hand with a developing community of people who responded to one another in their need. The Notting Hill Housing Trust and others have continued to make a great impression on the lives of many people. The Blenheim and Portobello Projects, two of those started by the Notting Hill Social Council, were the result, first of all, of the social application of the Christian Gospel. They were related to a community of people with concern for their neighbours.

We all felt the need for worship and biblical preaching in the Christian community. We were made aware in and through this community, of the opportunities and the thanksgiving, as well as the problems, which this life in the city provided. Ministry in the world was the counterpart of the Liturgy or 'piece of service' in the Christian community together in worship. John Robinson explains in *On Being the Church in the World* how this liturgy of the Eucharist is the Gospel in action. The word and the deed go together in worship and in life.

9

It was certainly our experience that the worshipping life of the Body of Christ, the Christian community, was part of the life of ministry and pastoral concern, that both plugged in to the divine nature of the Body and were earthed in the human aspect of the incarnation. For all the effort and work that went into the practical application of the Good News, there had to be that gathering in Holy celebration on the day of the Lord. For all the glory of the Festival occasion or the thanksgiving of worship, there had to be the participating in the actions of that Body of Christ in its daily duties and ministry.

John Robinson enlarges on the whole drama of the Eucharist in the world, in *Liturgy Come to Life*, which became a reality for us in Notting Hill. The actions of Jesus, and of us as we participate in the drama, spell out the meaning of discipleship and of being the body in the world. Jesus *takes* the bread and wine that is brought; he *blesses* or gives thanks for it; he *breaks* the bread and pours the wine and *shares* them out to all the company. Finally he *sends out* the people as the body to the world. A hymn, produced in Notting Hill, interprets this in discipleship and life:

### A Communion

He takes the bread that comes into his hands,
    The bread produced in oven, home and field.
He takes the daily bread of many lands,
    The daily life of those his life has sealed.

He lifts the cup in blessing with the bread;
    Thanksgiving for the wholesome life of God.
He blesses with his presence and his grace,
    Material for usefulness and food.

He breaks the bread, familiar in the sign;
    The homely act that speaks the family round.
A sacrifice far from a table spread;
    His body broken on the deathly mound.

He gives the bread and cup to all who come,
A sharing out of mystery and life;
The passing round to children who come home,
The vital fellowship in blood and strife.

He sends a broken body to the world,
A Church that holds his life within its own;
The evidence of blood and faith and hope,
To careless men and crowded, crushing town.

'The Church for Others', the World Council of Churches' report a few years ago on the missionary structure of the congregation, looked at what constituted Christian presence in our communities today. 'For centuries, the local congregation, made up of those living in a small, easily defined, geographical area, has been the basic unit of the Church. To affirm that Christian presence in modern life means the emergence of an increasing number of varying forms of church life, creates a crisis for the local church, since the restructuring of the churches cannot proceed effectively until the "parish" has become reconciled to this new fact.' The parish 'once represented the whole church, face to face with what was to all intents and purposes, for most people, the whole of life'. This is no longer the case. The areas still able to be served represent a small sector of life. The tendency is for many local congregations to withdraw into themselves, to care for the 'faithful' and to find justification for their life within themselves, instead of in their mission to the world. What this should really lead us to is not a withdrawal but an extension of the areas of our care.

Caring will be expressed in the work done daily, by so many of our people in the social services, in housing, welfare, probation service, personal work, teaching and in health services. Many Christian people are engaged in 'making people whole' and most of our churches have evidence of this kind of ministry among their people.

11

More of these should be representing their work in ministry, on the councils and committees of the church, and we should be making more space for them and their expertise.

Voluntary work will be only a part of that ministry, if a real part. The many community organizations in which our people can take their place include tenants' associations, community development committees, teams to run adventure playgrounds and play groups and clubs of all kinds. The variety of meetings on church premises form an important part of the contribution in ministry that the church can make. All our premises should be put thus, at the disposal of the community, for service and ministry. A caring church will therefore be engaged through its people and their daily work, through work by its people with local organizations in a voluntary capacity, and through work on its premises by its own people or others.

When Jesus takes the bread, he is receiving all the forms of life and ministry that we have to offer. Jesus takes what we give; he 'gets his hands on it' and makes it rich with his own life and love. The blessing or thanksgiving is the holding up in celebration of all the gifts and love and service that people have to offer. The blessing of God upon this and us turn the body or community into food and life for others. How much we need this kind of celebration, when we make 'whoopee' with all the potential of festival and worship and party and meal and social occasion, as the people of the Lord.

Being 'broken' is the way of sacrifice. There is no way to victory, no way of life for us or the community which does not go the way of giving and obedience to Christ. Part of the growing in community through worship and prayer and fellowship, is to re-shape and change the selfishness of man into the Christ-centredness of the body of Christ. A 'sharing' out is the experience of every passing on of forgiveness. The 'Peace' passed in worship,

12

the kneeling together of those with differences of race, background, colour and culture, who listen and learn from each other—'Is it not a sharing in the body of Christ?' To discover that sharing is to discover new life for old. Jesus shares out among us what we ourselves contribute, as with the loaves and fish, with his blessing and imprint of love upon it.

The 'sending out' has obvious meaning for the Christian community, but it should not be seen as going into a hostile and secular world. The process of secularization is one in which the Church must participate and learn. God is at work in this process and the mission of the Church is found in helping Christians to see that Christ is in the world before they go to it. Our task there is to be where he is, strengthening and upholding what we discern of Christ and rebuking and challenging what is opposed to him.

All the foregoing shows how important the worshipping Christian community is. Most of us cannot survive without the sustenance and strength from our gathering together with God in the company of his people. The enactment of our whole life which takes place in worship means that worship has to be real and valid and relevant and alive if our own daily life is going to reflect it. There is real renewal of Christian life for those who make the discovery of real worship and its power to change. It means a readiness and willingness to change in our attitudes to worship, instead of being held in the stereotypes of formal liturgy or so-called nonconformist freedom. Both of these become straight-jackets of the devil to resist all change and renewal! There must be real participation by all the people there. They should not just watch-up-front, as if they were in a theatre or cinema. The unfortunate serried ranks of seating of most churches does not help this and we need to have much more worship in the round, with seating that can move to allow freedom and participation. Teams of people always need

13

to take part in the conducting of worship to represent this full participation. Another aspect is a balance between order and spontaneity. Liturgical order will see that the various elements of the full worship of God are always there, including praise and thanksgiving, confession and meditation, God's word to us and our response, intercession and dedication.

One of the strongest arguments I know for the value of real Christian presence in the world, stemming from real community and real worship, is the life-changing power of that community life. If you look where real evangelism is taking place, you will find it in live Christian communities. By their very life they draw people to Christ. Doing the deeds of Christ means that people see his love and are drawn to him.

As with people engaged in their daily work, the Christian presence may not be tidily related to any one existing Christian community that gathers for worship on Sundays. The people who relate to one another in their ministry of work may come from several communities or none. Non-residential communities have to be seen as part of the life of the world and as needing as much care as residential ones. Commuters who spend a long time in the city, and professional people who find their communities in groups or associations, all need a different kind of centre of community. The artificial suburban community cannot provide a natural meeting place for such people. This is where the Ecumenical Centre, in whatever form, in the centre of urban population, located in central missions or down-town churches, should come into its own. There is a need to experiment in these forms of Christian presence in all our city centres. My experience of the Notting Hill Ecumenical Centre and the London Centre show how much can be done in caring and discovering new ways of work and mission and the understanding together of the meaning of the Gospel. One aspect of this is, of course, that it must be inter-denominational. The word Ecumenical relates to the whole inhabited world, but is used to describe the work and relationship between Christians of different backgrounds and denominations. It goes without saying that the body of Christ cannot be divided and our ultimate aim in being the body of Christ in the world is 'to be one. that the world may believe'.

The following chapters will demonstrate the ways in which the Christian community, however based, can exercise its pastoral ministry. In doing so, it must express a wholeness and a unity in itself which will enable the world to see the body of Christ. For this purpose, the more our local communities can be ecumenical or inter-denominational the better. Our love and care for one another is a necessary part of our being able to care for others.

## Questions for discussion

1. How does your Christian community combine the words and the deeds of Christ? Are they held together in proclamation and action?

2. Do you see the celebration of the Eucharist or Communion in your community as a working-out of the life of the body in the world? Is it only symbolic, or does the acting-out move into reality?

3. Does your Church as a community and as a building contribute to the life of the community round about? What do you know about Ecumenical Centres that relate to people not in a residential community?

4. Read 1 Corinthians 10, especially verses 14–17. What does this say about the need for unity in the body?

## 2 Sharing in Ministry

**The minister**

One of the biggest problems for ministry in the Christian community is the minister! We have built up an image over the years of the place of the clergyman, priest or minister, that makes him, or her, 'the person' of a community. He was 'the person' of a civic or cultural community in the rural parish. Since the parish concept has been overturned by the city and the conurbation, this 'person' has become associated with the local congregation in a special way and as having a special role.

Many congregations have tended to leave ministry to the minister, and even when they have been engaging in ministry they have not dared, or been willing, to call it that. The parson has therefore become the idol or the scapegoat for the Church; the tin-god or the Aunt Sally to be in turn elevated or knocked down. While this pre-occupation went on, the work of ministry was overlooked. A preoccupation with the ordained ministry does not lead to extensions of ministry.

A Church like the Methodist Church has done better than some in the use of 'lay people', but that very term emphasizes the distinction between 'real ministry' and a kind of 'makeshift ministry' as some people regard it. So the lay preacher and the lay visitor are not thought of in the same way as the ordained person. This is a corruption of the concept of ministry for which both ordained and non-ordained are to blame. Ministry is exercised by the whole community and the ordained person has her or his part to play in the whole, but it is only a part. No one person can exercise all the aspects of ministry that there are, nor can that person actually do all the work of ministering that needs to be done.

How little visiting would be done if it were all left to the parson! It would take the individual minister a year, doing little else, to visit properly all the families on the community roll of most local churches of average size.

It is a misconception when the parson is thought of as different, separate, a leader in the wrong sense—that is, not as a leader among others, but as one having an authority role. The minister, by virtue of his name and calling, is a servant; pastoral visitors and all the other people exercising ministry are also servants. The whole church in ministry and every member a pastor or minister would make a different image from that of the one shepherd and the flock of sheep. We have been misled by making the figure of Jesus, the Good Shepherd, fit our pastoral patterns. We need to think of people and a lot of under-shepherds if we are going to retain the pastoral metaphor, but we shall look again at this.

As the paid 'shepherds' decrease in number, or cannot be paid for in quantity today, we must see pastorship as being non-paid and part-time. Very little of the Presbyter-Coordinator's time may be spent on pastoral visitation. The pastor, whoever she or he is, is therefore on the same 'level' as the person seen or visited. The 'mystique', if there is one, is in being a representative person, representing, by the act, God and the Church.

### Presbyters

It will be seen that I go along with the view that ordained people should be called presbyters. This would get away from the 'Minister' idea on the one hand, creaming off ministry, and the 'Priest' concept on the other, which often sets the person apart in a wrong way. Certainly we could give a lead in this from the non-episcopal churches by calling our ordained people presbyters. It would help our people to see ministry in a different way.

The ministry of the Presbyter is described in Methodist terms in the report on 'Ordination' adopted by the 1974

17

Methodist Conference. Their 'authority' is in preaching the word and administering the sacraments (as a matter of order, not of faith). It is seen (on page 5 of the report —'Ordained to what?') to include various other functions which are shared by lay people, while not including all the functions to a high degree does not deny the ordination. 'In the office, the calling of the whole church is focused and represented, and it is their responsibility as representative persons to lead the people to share with them in that calling. In this sense they are the sign of the presence and ministry of Christ in the Church, and through the Church to the world.'

New and experimental ministries have been with us throughout the history of the Church and there are many examples today. It is right that we see ministry extending and expanding in many ways throughout the whole people of God and throughout the arena of the life of the world (*oecumene*). This is why Sector ministries have such a deep significance for the Church when properly understood and correctly used. The search for a role in ministry in new areas of life, is a learning and maturing process of ministry, and not only for the person concerned. The Church as a whole and especially the local Christian community has a great deal to discover and receive from the person in a Sector ministry.

The place of the 'Sector' minister, or the non-stipendary presbyter, is an important aspect of a new 'sharing in ministry'. The new discussion on 'auxiliary' ministry asks similar searching questions. Whereas financial demands are making it less likely to have an increase in paid, ordained ministers, 'sector', 'auxiliary' or 'non-stipendary' would allow us to have more. It is a theological question rather than an economic one and the theology is that all share in ministry and could well contribute their ministry to the life of the Church while being paid in other ways. A few full-time specialists in each diocese or district would be sufficient, and we could multiply ministry in local church and parish communities. The discussion about the 'sectors' is filled with hypocrisy and illusion. Are we really asking that ordained ministers should *only* do pastoral, preaching and sacramental work? If so, three quarters of the work now being done by ministers would have to be stopped. What about the cleaning, caretaking, duplicating, administration, printing, publicity, committee and postman's jobs, to name but a few, that are done by ministers? I would defend them as being part of the normality of life from which real ministry proceeds, but the point is that they are already in the sectors, with the connivance of the church. They spend part of their time on pastoral-sacramental work, as anyone in the sectors can and will do.

Many more retired people, many more people working locally in their own professions, and many more who are strongly committed to a form of ministry in their daily life, should be ordained, in order to increase the range of meaning of ministry for the Church. How devastating is a terminology that classes the tent-making ministry of St Paul as 'auxiliary' to a full-time one! The auxiliary ministry should be that of the full-time servants of the Church, who supplement, as far as they can, the work being done by those who share in the full ministry of the Church without being paid. Nothing would better emphasize that ministry belongs to the whole people of God and not to those who happen to be set aside and paid for doing it.

## Team ministries

These go a long way to a creative solution. On the team, for a particular area of a local Christian community, there can be two or three people who are now, in current parlance, 'in the sectors'. There can be several who are ordained, either as younger or older people, who pursue the work of ministry in their daily life and fulfil church work as and when they can. There can be one or two also, depending on the size of the community and the area and church buildings served, who are full-time and paid. They will be specialists in some form of ministry. Some of these patterns were suggested in *Towards a Radical Church* by Richard Jones and Anthony Wesson. For the most part there will be those who have specific work in ministry within the congregation and within the local community, who form part of the whole body of Christ. They will also share in team understanding and interpretation of work and theology, in decision making, in thinking and in structures.

Team Ministry is one of the great correctives of the individualistic approach to ministry. My experience of Group Ministry in Notting Hill has shown me how one has to change and correct one's own way of doing things for the common good. It is not easy for people to do this, especially when they have been trained and styled to an individualistic approach to ministry. It is for them and for the congregation a great learning process to a large and more wholesome concept of ministry. It is difficult to talk about 'our minister' if there is a team, or to blame the minister for a failing in ministry if there is more than one minister around! We say nothing about the fact that there is no (one) minister's wife! The process towards a fuller understanding of sharing in ministry is very valuable indeed. A further lesson is in an ecumenical team, which is the real team situation. Here there is a wonderful sharing, across the denominational boundaries, which allows ministry to be understood in still wider and deeper ways.

## Community in ministry

How do we engage the whole Christian community in ministry? It is important, first of all, to see that we know who the whole Christian community are! A well-kept community roll is an essential for the local church, but how many keep them properly and up to date? It should be one person's job to be responsible, under the Family Committee, or other structural equivalent, for the Community Roll. The description of the Community scheme practised in Notting Hill is found in chapter 9. A new flexibility, which was the concern of those who drafted the new structures in the Methodist Church, and was certainly the hope of the whole Church in receiving them, has to enable local schemes of ministry and pastoral care to fit into the whole. You cannot devise a system or structure to fit every place. If we are to be sensitive to the leading of the Spirit of God and to the needs of each situation, then there will be many different forms for different places. We must also demonstrate the all-inclusive nature of ministry within the company of God's people, by seeing that in every aspect it is represented in the courts of the Church. These 'courts' are so often dominated by the ordained, full-time ministers, or by people who are professional churchmen. The vagaries in ministry, which the Spirit is always producing, have to be allowed for and celebrated in the personnel who lead and in the structures of the Church.

**The shared ministry**
One of the problems for ordained clergy today arises out of the thinking on shared ministry. The questioning of their role and position means for some a sense of insecurity or a reaching out into other forms of service. This is not the place to go into detail about the care of ordained people (or any professional carers). I have dealt with this in a separate paper and the whole question is at the moment being considered by the Division of Ministries in the Methodist Church and of course by other Churches as well. We should indicate however that care for the carers is part of the ministry of the whole Church. We, the people, should see that there is proper pastoral support and guidance for our presbyters as part of our own ministry. A way of saying this is

that pastoral care should be 'circulatory' and not 'pyramidical'.

To continue the pastoral metaphor—shepherds are also sheep. A system has to be built up which enables every person having care for others to be cared for themselves. Social work practice can be looked at here.

The other aspect of the needs of pastors themselves is a deeply psychological one. It refers to the fact that most people need to be needed. The people who go into social work, or into pastoral-psychiatric caring, or into the ordained ministry of the Church, are often among those with particular need or inclination. It is not of course a fault or handicap in itself, but it carries with it the seeds of problems of need that are nurtured in over-concern, protectiveness or interference in other people's lives. Where this happens with pastors of any kind, it has to be watched carefully and corrected for the sake of the pastors themselves as well as for the sake of those to whom they seek to minister.

The problem of a guilt complex often arises with socially caring people. If we are not working hard, or see work that needs to be done not being done at that moment, we feel guilty. It is a complex which people should not induce in their pastors by expecting too much from them. If you comment, even in fun, about the fact that a minister or pastor is at leisure, when they might be 'working', you can do harm to their style of living and emotions. We should see that the carers have time to relax and not always be faced with problems. This is very much part of the shared ministry of the Church.

**Inter-dependence**

We all need to cultivate a correct attitude towards others' problems. It is not easy to find the right balance of objectivity and non-involvement in caring situations. Of course we need to be involved with people as part of the incarnational theology of the Gospel. What we also need to see is that we shall never do the best for people if we get so involved in their problems that they become ours as well. We then become so burdened, that we are also down and are not in the position to lift them up. It is essential to be able to stand aside, so that we can see things more clearly and help others to see things clearly too. Again, this means a willingness to refer people to others. You should never 'keep a case for yourself' when it is obvious that other counsels and expertise are called for. Our aim, especially in Christian community, is to find real inter-dependence. In a properly motivated and loving community, people will recognize both their need of others as well as what they can contribute to others. Unfortunately we often get stuck with dependence and independence. These characteristics are seen in people who cannot get along on their own and in those who mistakenly feel they can do without others. Those who are dependent, are so either because of their own inadequacies or because of mistakes in pastoral work. For these people it is important that we limit what we do so that we help them find themselves and their own strengths and weaknesses. There will be a few people who will always be dependent, but these will need professional care or statutory accommodation. Most people with whom we deal should be brought from dependence to inter-dependence, to a place where they can receive, but, from a position of finding their own identity, discover what they have to give as well. The independent person either mistakenly feels that he or she can do without others, or is naturally shy and unable to mix easily. It may be bravado rather than a sense of their own ability. The example required is of a mutually caring community where real needs are met for people in other people and where sharing with others is an enriching thing for the community as a whole.

**Questions for discussion**

1. Is 'minister' the best title for an ordained person in a community that should be exercising total ministry?

2. Examine the pastoral terms of the Bible from Psalm 23 to John 10 and see if they properly apply to pastors and people, especially in an urban setting.

3. What new forms of ministry do you see emerging in the next few years in this country? Have you any experience or information of new ministries here or overseas?

4. Is your Christian community geared to care for those who do the caring work, including the minister?

# 3 The Cure of Souls

## The meaning of the exercise

The traditional background to the 'cure' of souls has something of the range of meaning of the Latin *cura*. The primary sense of this is 'care' and is applied to tasks involved in, or to the experience of, carefulness concerning the object. There is however an additional, associated meaning of 'healing'. That is why 'care of souls', or pastoral care, is no adequate substitute for a 'cure' of souls. I am indebted in this understanding to Frederic Greeves in *Theology and the Cure of Souls* and to his own teaching. For those who have the time and inclination it is worth reading his book.

We still need a distinctive term for the pastoral attitude and function which can remind us that Christian care, like the love of God himself, must be for all, everywhere, and in all matters. The ultimate purpose of the Church, which is that of Christ, is the health which comes from God.

The word *soul* often conceals rather than illumines the nature of care and evangelism. The Greek thought ingrained in us sees a separation of body and soul, but Biblical thought, especially Hebrew, sees the soul as the whole personality. No other word, however, fully expresses the 'wholeness' of man, which is implied not only in the Bible, but also in modern psychology. The word 'soul' also reminds us of man's relationship to God, and his need for God. The twofold approach described by the word 'psychosomatic' (the interrelationship of mind and body) must for Christians become a three-fold approach. It is because the soul represents man's totality, that pastoral care extends (like mission) to every aspect of man's manifold existence. We misconceive the nature and needs of both body and mind if we forget what soul represents. The cure of souls therefore has its distinctive place alongside physical and psychiatric healing.

## Pastoral care

The image of pastoral care for most people is, I suspect, that of fat silly sheep! It is unfortunate because that implies the idea of green pastures, concentrated sheep farming and a lot of attention being given to lush, though foolish animals. We need to have in mind the rough hillside pastures, of Palestine and elsewhere, dry and bare and somewhat remote. There is the inattention which allows sheep to wander on the hills and get lost. The sheep are basically left to their own devices until they have to be rounded up, or when one of them gets into difficulties.

Interpreted into our life, pastorally, or in the city where urban images are necessary, care is not an invasion of people's private lives. There should not be an overconcern for their welfare, but a response to need on the one hand and a celebrating of joy and plenty on the other, when the green pastures do come along.

Care also relates to sheep together: getting on together and enjoying each other's company. The comfort and security of being together matters probably much more than any shepherding, occasional as it must inevitably be. The shepherd can be (though he ought not to be) an annoying intruder into the life of the flock, possibly to take the sheep to market! But we ought not to take the image and analogy of shepherding too far, for people are not sheep. The function beyond body and mind is involved and there is an individualism and independence of identity to be preserved and recognized more for human beings than for sheep.

The ministry of care ought to be more urban anyway, since the pastoral concept applies less and less for most of our church work. Perhaps we should cultivate the idea of street wardens or welfare workers, or community leaders?

The aim of the pastoral ministry, or the cure of souls, is of making people whole. Visiting then should have at least three aspects.

(a) There is the visiting of physically or mentally sick people to encourage and to cheer and to pray and help and heal.

(b) There is the enlarging of the mind in an educational sense, to truths and values of the faith. A teaching ministry is part of the whole pastoral exercise. Can you leave behind one new thought, or for that matter bring away one new thought? Can you change, even a little, a set prejudice or misapprehension? Can you leave information, newsletters, reports and suggestions and invite participation?

(c) There is also the calling to faith and to appreciation of the spiritual dimension of life. Commending the faith is not preaching at people, but is response to questions and problems and natural conversation, showing care and joy and love.

### What is the role of the pastor?

I think that the most important role is that of being a friend. This means that there will be no intrusion. Some people do not have many friends and some do not have a friend for a particular situation. Others need a friend with an objective and Christian viewpoint. To be a friend to people is to take the friendship of Jesus into their lives. The link between you, made over months and years by real friendship, means that when needs arise you are turned to for advice and counsel and aid and resources. Confidence and trust in the person who acts as pastoral friend does not come easily and of course must not be abused. It depends very much on sensitivity, kindness, concern and faithfulness, which sooner or later will earn

27

trust which people want to give, but can only give to
those who earn it in patience and love.

Involvement and detachment in pastoral relations is
not an easy balance to find, but it is very important. I
have known people, clerical and others, who get so involved with people and their problems as to be, in the
end, useless as friends or advisers. They become unbalanced and a problem themselves. Your relationship
must never involve you, on a pastoral level, in being so
close to a person that you cannot stand back from the
relationship. This is important ethically, it is equally
important pastorally. You must not make people dependent on you and you have no right to. Rather you must
do everything you can to prevent them being dependent
upon you, for their wholeness of life and cure. This
means that an ability to be detached is as important as
it is for social workers. You should not, except in
extreme cases and emergencies, take other people's problems to bed with you! When you have said your prayers
for them, and done what you could, you should be able
to go to sleep. You need, like everyone else, to come
home to your family, or in the case of non-family people
to friends, or to reading a book or listening to music or
watching the telly. An involvement which takes up the
majority of your spare time, except in the case of emergencies, is mistaken for you and for the people concerned. For instance, no one can take on more than two
or three concentrated interviews or conversations or
problem cases in a week, in addition to their ordinary
work. If you do find yourself doing that then cut it out
at once. You are human too—you are not God! Your
health of soul is as important as anyone else's, especially
when, as a pastor, you cannot do your work properly
and well if you are overwhelmed, overtired, over-
committed and over-involved.

Detachment needs to be found too in listening and
being objective and not rushing in with advice or with

ideas of your own on what to do in a particular situation. Counselling, in the non-technical sense, is following through this concept of detachment, related to trust and confidence.

(a) It is important first of all, in any problem situation, to sort out the facts and clarify the problem, by asking questions and sorting out the answers.

(b) It is then necessary to look at all the possible courses of action which the person himself or herself will be able to detail.

(c) In the course of examing these, a way often breaks through to the person concerned, without your having 'advised' anything.

(d) Spiritual counselling and direction may need more than that, but it is still better to let people discover truth for themselves, so that it is really *their* discovery.

## Deeper problems

In the course of visiting and conversation, we may discover much deeper problems of a psychological nature, or of a physical or mental kind, which we need to be able to recognize. Experience will tell you, or consulting with someone else about it will help you to see, that some people need the care of a doctor, or psychiatrist, and the sooner the better. We do wrong to prolong a relationship with us, when professional help is required. It is often the case that the Church accumulates people who are neurotic or psychologically astray. I do not say that cynically, I say it in a sense with thanksgiving, because where people with problems are, there the Church is known to be compassionate, receiving, accepting and resourceful. But we must be aware that what such people say and do, is not a reflection of their real spiritual need, nor of the real life and care of the Church, which they may castigate unmercifully! It simply means that people who are sick have to be carried by the Christian community and also, with care, handed over from time to time to other agents of healing. The Christian community is, or should be, in the vanguard of providing the care in community which hospitals and other social institutions practise.

Similarly, of course, some people may need the care or cure of the minister-presbyter-priest, in terms of their spiritual problems and dilemmas, if only because the ordained person formalizes for them the word that is given. As long as we have made sure that it is spiritual need and not a psychological one only, then there is a place, self-evident in our world, for the help and support of the Christian community, and the word of forgiveness and absolution. It may be required from the priestly part of our work, and every pastor has to be a priest sometimes. It is here that we need to take seriously our responsibilities of speaking the faith that is in us, of giving words of forgiveness from God, sometimes informally, but also sometimes quite formally in confession and absolution. We do no service to people or to the Church if we fail to recognize, from some nonconformist background or prejudice, the significance of real confession and absolution within the life of individuals or the Church.

There is also the need to pray with people that they may find healing and peace. It is often asked when prayer should be used in the course of visiting. My own criteria are as follows:

i. When it is natural to the visit and not forced, so that it arises out of the relationship, the conversation and the need.

ii. When it is requested by the person concerned.

iii. When someone is ill and/or dying, even when they are not aware of your presence.

iv. When the special situation they are going through (called below 'life-force situations') means that prayer really is required, for example at a bereavement, or in the joy at the birth of a baby.

### Life-force situations

My definition of such a situation, as the context in which the pastoral ministry takes place, is—a time or occasion in the life of a person or family when the real issues of being human, such as being born, living and dying, become for the person or family, the significant and all-important thing, and when lesser considerations are put aside as unimportant. At such a time of real issues, the Church and its pastoral people have their important part to play.

I find, incidentally, that occasions like this do not have to be sought after or looked for, but come to you. If the Christian community is open, loving, accepting and generally known to be helpful and caring, then people at such times will come to receive or to give of the life which is in Christ. I therefore believe them to be the really significant times for the Church's mission and ministry and pastoral care. It is these situations that are the bases of the other subjects of these chapters that follow and I will therefore simply mention them now.

I would list these situations as:

(a) The birth of a baby and the thanksgiving that surrounds it.

(b) Baptism and the preparation of the family for it.

(c) Family and school problems in adolescence.

(d) Preparation for Confirmation and Church membership.

(e) Changing home, school or work.

(f) Falling in love and preparation in relationships for marriage.

(g) A full and happy life and its celebration from time to time, especially at the Festivals of the Church year.

(h) Sickness in personal life or in the family.

(i) Breakdown of marriage or family relationship and divorce.

(j) Bereavement, death and funeral preparation.

(k) Added to these at every point, and almost in conjunction with them, the liturgical year and the rhythm of the birth, life, ministry and death and resurrection of Jesus.

We simply have to be ready to respond when such occasions arise and not despise the fact that people perhaps 'only' come at times like these. The readiness of a proper understanding among our pastoral visitors, and a preparing through months or even years of friendship making, together with proper organization and a continuing scheme of visiting, leads at such times to the real 'cure of souls'.

## Questions for discussion

1. What does the study of the following passages of Scripture (in the *N.E.B.*) teach us about the nature of man? Genesis 2:7 (living creature or soul); Exodus 12:4 (persons or souls); Judges 10:16 (endure no longer/soul grieved); Job 10:1–2 (sickened of life/soul weary); Psalm 23:3 renews life/restores soul); Matthew 11:29; Luke 12:19 (man/soul). *Note:* When the Hebrew speaks of 'heart' or 'mind' as distinct from 'soul' he is looking at the whole personality in a different way. In each case it is the whole person 'feeling', 'thinking' or 'being'.

2. Discuss the role of the pastor and the questions of involvement and detachment.

3. What is your experience of prayer with people who are sick and the healing ministry of the Church?

4. How have you found people's attitudes change in the life-force situations listed above?

## 4 Birth and Beginning Again

### Home and community background

I wonder how many young couples ask the question: 'What sort of a home is our child coming into?' The need to teach young people the theological importance of really preparing for another life coming into the world cannot be over emphasized. It is not easy to make time and opportunity before the baby actually arrives, but some good pastoral visitors might be able to do this well.

Perhaps there is no better time than Advent, which shows us theologically the need to prepare for the coming of a child, and the liturgical aspect of preparing for Christmas with Advent candles and calendar, Advent preaching and the like, are good teaching influences too. We were expecting our first two daughters (born in January) during Advent, and I remember the impression it made upon me of waiting and preparing for a child to come. The expectations of those who wanted and waited for Jesus and were ready for his coming are very interesting, especially when you note their simplicity and devotion (see Luke, chapters 1–2). Advent is a cycle that brings a baby along and birth is a cycle (rather than a stork!) in the lives of people that brings a baby. Because of the life-force situation of a birth, people are willing to think and to listen, unless there are connotations like 'unwanted pregnancy', 'family disapproval', 'unmarried mother'. Then there is still a fair amount of preparation and upheaval and emotion pouring in, and the need for pastoral care is evident. Every child has a birthright and part of it is that we, as parents, examine ourselves. Perhaps we should have a service for parents preparing for a baby to come.

It is often a catastrophic change to have a small baby

33

arrive! New habits and new methods of organizing life in the home are required. Attention changes from the couple to the baby, and from one another to the baby. Jealousy, irritation and other emotional changes take place which can mean pastoral problems and needs.

It can also mean questions, perplexity and mothers who are theologically attune! A number of people, always in my experience women, come for a mixture of the 'Churching of women' and the 'Thanksgiving of mothers'. Perhaps we ought to encourage more real thanksgiving and celebration and provide worship at least once a year for parents and children to make that kind of thanksgiving, as at an annual Baptismal Roll service. A lot of superstition surrounds birth, and parents, many of them unable to cope in a religious sense with all the deep issues raised, are often criticized for not knowing what they are about in coming to present the child. Who does know? Should not the Church be much more critical of itself and its own responsibilities?

## The place of infant baptism

I want us to see, first of all, baptism as it is associated in the minds of most ordinary parents, in a community, who bring their child along. There will be superstition; there will also be genuine faith and thought; there will be real thanksgiving and a turning to the Church. We all come across strange reasons why people come for baptism of a child, such as the belief that something may happen to it if it is not 'done'. While we must obviously try to change such ideas, we should be no longer willing to scoff at such 'superstition'. When we criticize superstition, what do we mean by it? Is it a belief in the numinous? Is it a belief in another world than this one? Is it non-Christian or un-Christian? Is it not rather something which goes back into the history of a race or tribe or culture and speaks of inherent religion? I know that this is not necessarily a good thing, but it is there in all of us, and needs to be recognized and accepted, as young children brought to Jesus are accepted. But is it right to bring families to baptism if they do not know what they are doing? Do we know what we are doing in baptism (infant *or* believers) or in any sacrament for that matter? If I find it difficult to say in words what I mean by the sacraments, how can I blame, or deny the coming, of a person with no theological training? 'I feel it is right', said a young woman to me a few months ago. I do not know how better to say it myself.

The sacrament of baptism is certainly nothing to do with what the child *does*. It is salvation by faith, not by works, and the faith is that of the parents and the Church. Perhaps if there is any blame to be attached it is at the door of churches who fail to live up to promises they should make on behalf of the family and the child. I see baptism supremely as an exercise in belonging. The baptism of Jesus was a theological statement about his belonging to the rest of humanity, of being one with them in their humanness. The baptism of our children at an early age is therefore a sacramental incorporation into the Body of Christ, and you cannot be too young for that. At the same time it is an important act of incorporation for the parents, who, in a very real way, do their own baptism and beginning again at this point.

If you like to put it this way, it is the baptism of the Holy Spirit which is the essential baptism, and for that infant baptism is a preparation and believer's baptism is a confirmation. They should be, but they may not be. It may be that the child baptized does not go on to full life in Christ, and is always at the partial stage. It may be that those baptized in later life also do not have a faith confirmed within them, but neither fact should deter us from baptism itself, which is a sacrament of community, of belonging together in Christ, out of which a whole life of Christian faith may be possible for the person and the family and friends.

## The pastoral practice of baptism

I find that baptism is a supremely important event for every family and a time when people are most willing to listen and to make promises. There is opportunity for the people (parents and church) to recall their own baptism, sometimes with confirming results.

One of the things that needs to be got over to everyone is the relationship between the individual family and the Christian family of the Church. Baptism is a community sacrament and belongs to the whole family of the Church, not to the individual family. It is not an affair the family can have on its own, in the afternoon, in some quiet spot with the parson. That is not baptism!

I see the practice of infant baptism as a pastoral matter, making strong and binding relationships with the Church. You make good things possible for the child within the family of the Church. You cannot bring the baby without bringing yourselves and being involved. It is therefore a sacrament of Christian community, as Holy Communion is. It is essential that the Church is very much involved, with its Community Leaders or Baptismal Roll visitors and the rest. Visits and acquaintances made then are important for a long time. We make a practice of explaining the service in simple terms, indicating what promises have to be made, asking questions and finding out the resolve and intentions of the parents. We have also made it a firm practice to explain to the congregation constantly what it is about and what they are doing and promising to do. The service order that we have used makes the congregation say together a long statement about their intentions and promises and responsibilities.

The follow-up to the service is equally important, for the minister who conducts the service and for the Community Leader introduced to the family and being in touch with them thereafter. Some people feel that the visit to church by the family and their interest in the church at that point means nothing; that they may not come again, except on special occasions despite all the work of passing on information and visiting. Nevertheless, it is the responsibility of the Church from that time onwards through its representative pastors to care for the child and the family as far as it is able, and to try to see that in the Beginners Department and in the rest of its Junior Church life, the open acceptance and responsibility is there. We entered into a solemn covenant or sacrament and made our vows before God. Any failure, pastorally, to involve the child in the full life of the Christian community is as much as anything the Church's failure. We ask, in our services, for the parents to be there to make the promises. Godparents are not required, but we welcome them and should give them a significant place. If the parents do not fulfil the promises of a Christian home, a life of example and encouraging the child to come to School and Church (and what parents among us really do?), so much the more for the Church to do.

## Growing up

What a painful process it is too! Have you finished growing up? Coming to maturity, to the full and whole person, does not come easily or quickly. The list of problems of adolescence can be a long one. Do we not find they are really our problems all along, for being made whole is a life-time's work very often? There is the 'finding your feet', wanting to establish your independence, your own 'rights and freedom'. Freedom usually does not take into account the rights of others and it is not thereby true freedom, as we live to discover. All this brings the young person into conflict with authority in any form. We, and the Church, are authority figures. A great amount of pastoral work is required alongside the young person if that is possible; and the relationships with youth leaders and teachers is so important here. There is an equal amount of work to be done with the family, as it finds its place questioned and rejected. Again it is important to be as objective to the situation as possible, and to learn about the way in which people react and go through these periods of life. If you too easily accept the arguments of one side or the other, you cannot then keep the full confidence of the other party. The job of holding the ring while the arguments take place, and then picking up the pieces afterwards, can be an enervating experience. It is of course a vital time for the family. It can be given a sharp rift or break at this point, sometimes it has to, and it will affect the family for ever after. The young person needs great care, in spite of apparent aloofness on her or his part. Amid the obstinacy and foolishness, there may be no other way for them to find and accept a path for themselves.

All the above means that it is even more vital now than ever, with the increased pressures of society, for young people to have right choices and right attitudes put before them by the time the disruptive growing up process begins. The vital years now are from five to ten. Assuming of course that love and care and encouragement have been given them, they will be in the Junior Department! When young people now get to eleven or twelve, they are right on the edge of their ability to listen and learn for a period. Unless you are convinced that this is the right way for them to learn, or unless they are convinced that they want to learn this way, you may as well give up! Not that you should! Relationships are then more important than teaching. As far as faith and ideals are concerned, they will have needed to be brought up in an atmosphere of what is right, and even if they reject it at the growing up stage, they will have something to which to come back later.

The experience of conversion in youth or childhood needs to be touched on here, but will be dealt with more fully in chapter 8. The impressionable age of early teens is a time when an appeal to faith and discipleship should be made. This does not mean to say that I think there should be a battering of the young person in an evangelical zeal which can destroy a proper response of faith. Nor should it be a matter of taking advantage of impressionableness. Yet at a time when the world is opening out in challenge, and demanding in all other ways allegiance or answers, it would be wrong not to put the case for Jesus Christ as a leader and saviour. I think that, as with all challenges for discipleship, it should be at special times, associated naturally with the Gospel and the life of Jesus in the Christian year. For instance, Lent, Passion and Good Friday, leading up to Easter, are supremely relevant and meaningful for discipleship. To ask for response all the time, is to defeat the purpose of asking a 'timely' question.

In a sense, the 'bringing up a family' problems of the individual family, are repeated in the complex life of the Church. The young person will either rebel and leave 'home' and not want the word of the older people and go on his own way, or, if something meaningful has come home to him, he will latch on to the Christian community and to Jesus. The growing-up process in the Christian faith can mean that people will not take our word for it. The authority, in that sense, of the Church, has gone. It must be their word, their own discovered word. All we can do as a Christian 'family', is to see that the right things are said and done in the early growing period. After that the young person may come to realization when they come to one of the other life-force situations.

Confirmation, commitment or Church membership are the normal liturgical or Christian community terms to equate with the growing up period. It is said that there is a lack of willingness to commit oneself today. It may be that people do not find many things that constrain them to meaningful commitment. There is other commitment taking place all the time in some degree. It may be to home and family and friends, or to peer group, or gang or club, or sport or school, or even jobs and service. Perhaps the secret is in trusting and belonging and feeling part of what is happening, not observing something as an outsider. Real love and trust, as in marriage, involves commitment. If people do not therefore commit themselves to the Church, it must be for the reason that they have not been shown love personified. Perhaps one of the prime functions of the Christian community is to show such love and sacrifice that the way of Jesus is made quite plain. This will bring trust and commitment in its own good time.

### The changes in life are life-force times

I simply mention in passing the changes that occur in starting school or going to a different school, or starting work, or changing the place where you live, going to another town altogether, or in changing job/vocation. These changes do have pastoral significance. Visiting is usually done then to indicate interest and concern, but it is also important theologically at points where people are open to the issues of life and need to have a word of truth and love spoken to them. Another way of saying this would be that there are sacramental points of life, even where all life is felt to be sacramental, and then occasions have symbolic significance. We should perhaps encourage people to take part in a sacrament at those times, as at Baptism, Confirmation, Marriage and Holy Communion, as beginning again.

### Questions for discussion

1. What has been your experience of the change and significance of the coming of a child into your home?

2. How can you follow up the pastoral opportunities of baptism and confirmation?

40

3. What part does the worship of the Church play in making people feel that they belong?

4. Do we welcome change in growing up to maturity, or do we resist it as breaking up the relationships of the past? How can we help one another to progress towards maturity?

# 5 Love and Marriage

**What is love?**

In talking of life-force situations of birth and baptism, and all that they mean for family life, it is natural that love should be hovering in the wings. You may feel that talking to young parents and counselling them for marriage is a prerequisite to counselling for baptism. It doesn't always work out like that. There is a real sense in which an understanding of marriage does not come at the beginning of married life or before having children. We go on learning what marriage is about all our married lives. The alternative which some adopt today of a trial marriage is quite illogical, because it is the actual commitment in marriage which changes the whole scene. Commitment means love and trust, and conversely love and trust mean commitment.

From the growing-up stage, young people's eyes are on love and marriage. It is seen then as a romantic ideal with an ideal partner, and the behaviour of adolescents who prepare for this in their physical and emotional lives must be seen with understanding and the right kind of pastoral care. All kinds of confusing emotions are held together when we think of love. It means tenderness and holding hands; it means kissing in the moonlight; it means having sexual relationship and union with all that that involves physically and emotionally; it means caring and giving; it means mother-love and parents/children; it means putting someone else first; it means commitment and trust; it means self-sacrifice; it means the sublimity of a perfect relationship; it means the great power behind all things; it means the grace and goodness of God. Any of these can conflict with others, which may mean a breakdown in relationships, a breakdown of personality and psychological stability, or a breakdown of faith.

So pastoral care, where it is involved, of people in love, or having been in love and fallen out of it, or wanting to be in love, is understanding of this life-force situation with a vengeance! (Well not always with vengeance!) Hate, bitterness, hardness, frustration and immaturity are the results of an inability in some form to grow in love.

It is not easy for people to start from the Bible and the Christian faith in this, but perhaps we should do that to find perspective. *Cheseth* is the Hebrew word meaning 'covenant love' or loving-kindness, and translated 'love' in English—e.g. God's love worked out in Hosea in the imagery of a man and an unfaithful wife. *Ahaba* means love as unconditional choice or choosing of someone to be the beloved (Deuteronomy 7—God choosing Israel, not because she is a great nation, but of sheer love). *Chen* (pronounced Kane) is the kindness or favour, free and undeserved, which we think of as 'grace', but also translated love in the Old Testament. In the New Testament the Greek words are *Agape*—gracious love and *Phileo,* to be a friend. All that variation and richness in the Bible has to be contained in the one English word, love. It is no wonder we get confused. How then can we define love for this purpose of human relationships, between men and women, men and men, women and women—because we are thinking not only of the Jacob and Rachel relationship, but also of David and Jonathan and Naomi and Ruth, etc.? I would only begin a definition and invite you to continue to think about it. It is a natural relationship of choice and affection which reflects in human life something of the meaning of the whole of existence. To love fully is to be fully human and this is as natural to human life as breathing and eating and sleeping. What we are looking at therefore in pastoral terms is the recognizing of what goes on, or should go on, as the natural processes of human relationship and what goes on when these natural relationships between people for some reason do not obtain.

## Problems and opportunities of sexual relationship

(a) Everyone needs a loving relationship, which means a choice which involves loving-kindness, not an act of convenience. The relationship should involve the whole personality, physically, mentally, emotionally and spiritually.

(b) The practise of sex, in terms of relationships and intercourse, is an essential part of love. Outside marriage it is difficult to find real fulfilment which does not conflict with Christian ethics.

(c) As far as homosexuality is concerned, the Church has been very unhelpful and unkind. People by nature homosexual have not had useful counsel from the Church as to finding a proper functioning homosexual relationship, if that is their natural inclination. We have to discover with them how this relates to their Christian faith, and at all times give complete acceptance within Christian community.

(d) Full enjoyment and full maturity can be found in a full experience of deep heterosexual love and relationship. It is part of maturity to find one's personality incomplete in the individual, made real in the other person. Maturity may also mean the ability to cope with life as an individual who cannot have that kind of relationship.

(e) Meeting the needs of those who do not find natural fulfilment is very much a pastoral opportunity. The physical or psychological needs may make such people either demanding or else withdrawn and emotionally unstable.

## Pastoral theology of relationships

Within the family, fatherhood is not always a happy concept for people. The role and rights of women and children have to be taken into account in ways in which they were not in Victorian society. The literalist view of certain Bible passages have been a great hindrance to Christian thinking and practice. We can learn a lot from Jesus' attitude to women even in the restricted society of his day. We can learn still more from the liberation which is in Christ. In the days of working wives and 'liberated' young people, the man who expects to lord it over his household (as some still do) is both a fool and a knave! A sharing in the work and chores of the family is necessary for father and children. Christian relationships mean that these lessons have to be learned and we are still dependent on mothers to teach them. They may do so by refusing to cook meals, or insisting on effort by sons as well as daughters, in order that masculine inadequacy is not perpetuated in the next generation. She may do it by moving out of the double bed when father is not responsive to any other incentive. This is not a plea for Women's Lib., it is a plea for Christian theology. We are not made whole until we give and receive the lessons which the family can teach.

What of the single person, or those whose family life does not come up to these expectations? The single person has advantages as well as disadvantages, but needs to relate to people in other ways. It is a learning process which Christian sensitivity on all sides must encourage. The person who matures as an individual is sometimes better balanced and able to deal with situations with which others cannot cope. There is the problem of the inadequacy of widows or widowers, solved the hard way by others. The extended family can be an answer, but the usual problems of living together can be even more prominent here. Associations of people meeting on a regular basis or living in community is not always the answer for those who deeply need close ties and the warm, physical proximity of someone to love and be loved by. When one has to say that there is probably no answer except in

45

Christian community, that is not to be callous, but to be realistic and to set the aims of the community high. It may be that warmth and love and peace have still to be explored there.

Our Christian faith and pastoral theology show us several things. In the first place we have to be sensitive and tolerant of people who tend to be more difficult and demanding than others. This applies to some who are single, to the widow, the divorcee, the childless or the unhappily married. Sensitivity will take us sometimes to realism and trying to help people to independence and security. As relationships are the most important things that happen in people's lives, and loving kindness and grace are so much aspects of our faith, it is part of our job to see that we provide for deep friendships, as part of community care. We should not rule out without careful consideration, the Christian possibility of living together outside marriage.

*Koinonia* is the New Testament word for communion or fellowship and holding things in common and a sharing of gifts. I think we all know something of this from experience of what the Holy Spirit can do in producing a marvellous understanding and affection between us. There is concern and care for each other, joy in one another's company, and a power and strength which develops through a common faith and love and peace and hope. It is basically this which is the 'support' in the social work sense, for the pastoral worker and the visitor of the Church. We must not forget the people who do not find this even in a loving community; we must not take our common life for granted but cultivate it as part of the meaning of caring love.

## And so to marriage

Preparation for marriage is a significant time of life-force proportions. Ideally there should be a series with a group of couples and others as well as the minister-pastor. Some couples, apart from those committed to the life of the Christian community, visit the parson with trepidation in case they should get a lecture on Christian behaviour. Not all are receptive to the kind of 'course' we would like to give. Let me say what I do and say.

(a) It is necessary still, in some cases, to talk about family planning (especially if there are children already!) and it is sometimes required to speak of their treatment of one another in sexual relations.

(b) Some men, by nature and appetite, are greedy for sex. This means that soon after marriage, or at times when the woman is unable to respond, there is hurt and burden upon her, which is sometimes little short of rape. On top of an otherwise busy life in which she has to do a lot of things in the home which the man should do, she is exploited physically.

Some women also need to understand that their desire, or lack of it, for sexual relationship, either at particular periods or altogether, should be tempered by an understanding of the needs and temperament of the man.

(c) Marriage is not a short sprint, it is a life-time of learning. It is perhaps a good thing to give books to help with family planning and sex techniques, in order that people can work together for an improvement of relationship over a long period, so that there are objectives always in view.

(d) Something should also be said about the subject which comes second in the marriage break-up stakes, that is money. One must say to people that, as a couple, they are as one as far as money is concerned and have to work it *all* out between them. It is no more right for a woman to use her housekeeping as a fund where the surplus can be used to get things for herself, than it is for the man not to let his wife know what he earns and only give her a fixed amount to deal with, keeping the rest for himself. In these days when both partners are working, all the money from both should go into the common pool or banking account and allocated to all the things and funds that are required including personal cash.

(e) Something has to be said about 'in-laws', about the sober realities of marriage, about the great problems that children will bring.

I feel that the best way to deal with all this in Christian community is to have an ongoing group of senior pastoral people to which those seeking marriage preparation can come.

### Sex, marriage and the Church

With Paul, the Church as a whole has been guilty of denigrating marriage and elevating celibacy. This I believe to be both a heresy on the Church's part and the cause of a lot of trouble for individual Christians brought up on this thinking. Sex, far from being sinful, is a gift of God, but like all other gifts has to be rightly used with due concern for other people. If the soul is the whole personality, then part of the soul's natural functioning is in sexual relationship. It was Paul who took one of the theories from the Old Testament, of how sin came into the world (cf. Genesis 3 with Genesis 4:7 and Genesis 6:1–7 and Genesis 8:21, to note three other of the theories). He thus overemphasized the associations of nakedness, flesh and sex and made sin to have a sexual content. Some people need clearing from the kind of guilt thus built up, and being made into whole persons, who enjoy their sex life in its true context.

### Divorce and re-marriage

(a) More people today are opting out of marriage or seeking divorce. This sad fact is often due to a lack of real growing up in marriage. As in all other life situations, you cannot stay in the early stages, or in patterns which were right at twenty, but cannot be right at thirty-five or fifty. Learning from mistakes, working hard at relationships and much more effort and selflessness are required to make the marriage the whole and wonderful thing it can become.

(b) This does not mean that divorce is not liberation for some. Mistakes are made in getting married, and some people do need to be relieved of the condemnation to sorrow and hurt all their lives because of an early mistake in marrying too young or marrying someone quite unsuitable. Not that we have a right to happiness all along the line. We marry for better or worse, and the 'worse' needs to be taken seriously by more people as part of a real commitment.

We must not look at divorce as a sin. The Bible teaching ascribed to Jesus is debatable. I think that the spirit of Jesus' teaching would not require life-long agony for two people from a wrong choice, or within a separation which cannot be taken further by either party.

(c) The teaching of the Church can be hypocritical, as when Canon Law says one thing and the Anglican priest wishes for another and sends the couple seeking re-marriage within the Church to the Methodist minister. Some serious debate is required to see if there is not a better way for the health of churches and people. Divorce, properly recognized, should be part of the Church's healing ministry. This includes re-marriage within church, where it is evident that repentance and innocence and the desire to begin again are involved. To prevent someone marrying again, when there is real chance that happiness may come from the second marriage, and there is desire on the part of the couple concerned to get married in church, would seem to be contrary to the spirit of Jesus.

(d) In terms of pastoral caring, it is usually a much more serious time for the two people who come, sometimes after bitter experience, than it is for the young couple who come, rather blind to life, to marriage vows. My experience of most proper attempts of this kind, is that people are deeply grateful for another chance and very concerned indeed to make a 'go' of it. I think they should be helped and blessed at such times and given any support possible by the Church.

## Questions for discussion

1. Look up in a concordance the use of the words in the Bible translated 'love', 'loving-kindness', 'grace', etc. How do they help us to define love within the Christian faith?

2. Compare the problems of relationships in early Christian communities with those in our own. With the immanence of 'the end', Paul advocated a platonic friendship—see 1 Corinthians 7. It was he who made the classic non-quote of all time: 'It is better to marry than to burn with desire'! Can he be excused in the context? What relationships are allowable?

3. What is the best way of dealing with the pastoral problems created by sex, love, marriage and family relations, in the Christian community? Can some pastors be appointed to deal with these particularly?

4. Examine the question of divorce and re-marriage. Has it affected anyone known to you? Has the Church helped in any way?

## 6 Sickness and Health

**From marriage to the full life**

The title of this chapter is one of the promises of companionship and relationship made in the marriage service. Wholeness of life is something which is attained through difficulty and pain. Indeed within marriage itself problems and pain faced together are part of the discovery of fullness and wholeness. The question of the time and care you give to a sick or aged relative is a problem with marriage. There are times when a decision has to be taken between looking after someone else, or following your own career, or getting married. The decision is seldom clear cut, but people do need helping through such decisions. Some measure of an answer can be found if you consider that there should be usually one special relationship in life (apart from the intrusion of death) to which you should give up everything else. There are other lesser relationships which may spoil your life and other people's, if you consider it your responsibility to give everything to them as well. As an example of what I mean: a wife may consider it her full responsibility to look after a sick husband, but should not perhaps give full-time concern to a sick father, to the detriment of her own family. Everyone cannot have exclusive rights on our time and energy and life and responsibility. The corollary of that is of course that we should not make excessive demands on our families and friends, when they have more immediate concerns. There must be a time when, if we have faith and love and courage, we will say, 'I will not trouble them further'.

One other general point about caring for others in sickness is the need not only in a social sense but in a Christian sense, to develop community care. This relates to mental troubles, to ex-psychiatric patients, but also to chronically sick and ageing people. Our Christian pastoral theology will lead us to work for and to establish proper community patterns of caring that relieve individuals where possible of overwhelming burdens.

## What is health?

You will remember that 'soul' in the biblical sense means the whole personality. When we are talking about health therefore, we mean the proper functioning and well-being of the whole personality. It follows that true health requires well-being in the spiritual, social and mental sense as well as in the bodily sense. People will not find real health without the emotional, rational and spiritual aspects of their lives being properly catered for.

Wholeness, or bringing to health, or curing, is related in the New Testament to the Greek word *to save*. It is the word used for instance in Luke 8:48: 'Your faith has saved you', which is translated 'cured' or 'healed' or 'made you whole'. Making whole in this sense is part of the process of salvation or deliverance. Health as wholeness is therefore a helpful definition. One can see the important relationship, well recognized today, between Christian healing and the work of the doctor or psychiatrist. The healing processes of the Christian community and the cure of souls in pastoral/priestly care, need always to be taken into account.

One other word which requires looking at briefly here is the word 'peace'. The Bible definitions of *Shalom* (Hebrew) and *Eirene* (Greek) lead us to synonyms like wholeness, prosperity, fulness of life, maturity, completeness, all of which have great significance to the concept of health. Peace is not merely a state of mind in the individual, nor an absence of war in the world, but much more a social concept of what life can and should be like for all people in the Kingdom of God.

## Suffering and sin

One of the most intractable problems of theology, and certainly of pastoral theology, is that of suffering and of its relationship, if any, to sin.

Pain, suffering and ill-health are the constant encounter for pastors. All people have to endure these in themselves or someone else as an apparently integral part of life. This is not the place to deal with the whole theological question, although this in some part has to be grasped by those who work pastorally, as the question will be put to them in some form sooner or later. Sufficient to say here that there are positive aspects as well as negative ones; that while individual or collective sin is responsible for a lot of pain and suffering, it does not account for all of it as far as we can see. The other thing that needs to be said is that a theology which does not take into account the Cross of Jesus, and its constant theme and place in Christian life, will not find an answer for those who suffer.

We need to deal, in some people, with *guilt and sin*. Much suffering occurs, in some people, not through physical pain and disease but through feelings of guilt and 'sin-sickness'. Guilt may have come from something done which was wrong, or thought to have been wrong, and will go on weighing down for ever, unless something is done to relieve it. It is of course a quite proper thing that guilt or feeling of guilt should be the reaction to wrong done. We should not take the peculiar attitude that guilt is in itself misplaced. Our attempts to get rid of guilt in people should be because they cannot go on carrying it without detriment to the whole of their life and health. Forgiveness by other people and the forgiveness of God, declared to people like this, may be essential. We may do this by a proper statement or formal declaration of absolution. We must also go on to encourage a change of life as a positive way through, making good the wrong which has been done. There is a place for penance when it is seen to be the proper act of a penitent soul.

Although doubt is not in the same category, it should perhaps be mentioned here, as it causes havoc in some people's lives. This is not so much by its own philosophical questioning as by the feeling that some people have that it should not be there. It is really a guilt feeling about doubt. Doubt is a healthy thought process, without which much of the prophetic and other writing and thinking of the Bible and the Church would not have been done. We need to help people to see that doubt is not unnatural to the thinking, developing mind and life, and can lead to new thinking and faith. In this sense guilt which is resolved can also be a saving, cleansing and renewing experience.

A special problem which pastors come up against sometimes is the feeling by some people that they have committed the 'unforgiveable sin'. The idea of the 'sin against the Holy Spirit' is quoted as if it speaks of their own state. It is unlikely that anyone who is so conscious of their sin is in the position of having sinned against the Holy Spirit! This sin, in New Testament thought, is the denial of truth and love when it is seen and experienced. Very often therefore the person who feels he has committed this sin is covering a religious mania or mental disorder. If people cannot feel their guilt removed by a declaration of a priest or pastor, and hear at that point the good news of God's forgiveness, it may certainly mean that a Christian psychiatric opinion is called for.

A sense of sin is inculcated in some Christian theological teaching by the conflict between law and gospel, based on some of Paul's writings and descriptions of his own experience. (See Romans 7, for example, for the spiritual dilemma of not being able to do the good, and doing the evil which he does not want to do. He goes on of course to declare the Gospel of God's saving grace and deliverance.) There are some people who do not get through easily to a natural acceptance of God's saving and healing way. A sense of sinfulness is constantly with them and can de-humanize their lives. Some forms of this extreme puritanism can exhibit real lack of wholeness or health.

## Psychiatry and mental problems in pastoral practice

This is not a definitive statement about psychiatric methods of specialists. I give rather some guidelines for the ordinary visitor-pastor, in the dimension of wholeness from the mental aspect.

(a) We will all come up against 'difficult' people. Their difficulties (and ours) may be due to a 'cussedness' of character and an unwillingness to co-operate or listen, or to have anything to do with the Church at some points. While psychologists may want to discern reasons in the background of people, some at least will come under the heading of 'ordinary' sinfulness.

There are some people, however, who are neurotic, having some nervous disorder, related either to their temperament or their upbringing, which causes them to be extremely sensitive. This may show itself in depression, or in vacillation from depression to elation, or in criticism of other people, or in feeling a lack of care and attention, or feeling persecuted or badly treated by life. A number of people like this are today in the care of a doctor, or are on drugs, or having psychotherapy. If they are not, and are in the Christian community, we need first the help of an understanding G.P. It is not for us to try to work out their trouble, because the healing work of the world is also part of God's own healing. We tend to carry a number of neurotic people in a Christian community and it is right that we should. We need not take too seriously what they say about the community, or we shall find that the unbalanced neurotic view is dominating, rather than being supported by, the community. The people concerned are often quite unable to deal with their problems. They see things as what is being done, or not being done to them, by others.

(b) Some mental disorders or breakdowns are immediately discernible. While it is obvious that such people need and must have specialist treatment and care, there is also a very real place for community care and pastoral concern, to enable them not to feel estranged from others, and able to come back easily into normal living, as quickly as possible. Health here has its important community context.

We must not play with psychological theories because we happen to have read some psychology. This is a real temptation to Christian pastors. The prime rule in all such pastoral practice is, whenever you can, to refer to someone else more experienced, or with specialist knowledge. Because Pastoral Counselling in a technical sense takes a lot of time and effort and objectivity, through proper training, it is a mistake to get involved unless you are going to be properly trained, or take up full-time work in it.

You, as a visitor, may well be the first person to notice that something is wrong with a person. In which case you need to know what to do. If you cannot recognize symptoms of a disorder, get hold of someone who does, and then be able to refer to a doctor, psychiatric centre or social worker, or indeed to a priest/pastor when this is required.

(c) We must say something about the need of people under pressure today. Depression and worry and anxieties of all kinds may bring a breakdown or mental illness. There are several things which, as a community, we should do.

i. We need to provide in the Christian community a place of worship and loving relationship where healing and help and hope are found.

ii. There also need to be groups of people meeting to talk and share their problems and experience and in love find strength in one another.

iii. There needs to be the possibility of relationships

with pastoral visitors, lay or ordained, that can provide a deep, confidential and helpful concourse of love and faith. Such a relationship can be costly to the pastor/counsellor, but it is part of the need of a number of people, often professional social workers themselves, in their sensitive response to the world today.

iv. We need ourselves to know our faith and be able to 'preach' of the hope and love of the Gospel. This 'preaching' will not of course be so much from the pulpit, but it needs to be shaped in our minds and lives in declaratory form, as if it were to be preached.

## Visitation of the sick

I have an old book published in 1897 entitled *Peace, the voice of the Church to her sick*. Even though the language is archaic, I feel that to be a helpful title, and the emphasis on practical detail is also to be welcomed for most of us who are pastor-visitors. The fact that the great word *peace* is used, is an indication, as we have seen already, that this is a social context within the Christian community. Peace is more than a greeting, it is an environment of good wishes, such as is involved in intercessory prayer. If we simply bear in mind when we visit the sick, that it is peace we come to bring, we shall have done good.

Sometimes *prayer* is possible and right; and you can see the suggested guide lines in chapter 3. Occasionally *absolution* is required. *Blessing* and the use of the laying on of hands, or a kind of peaceful communication with the hands, is often appropriate. I find that I tend often to use my hands when visiting the sick. This is sometimes simply holding their hands, while I am talking with them. I also find that resting my hand on the head of the person concerned, either in prayer, or as a parting act of 'blessing', seems right. I believe we can thereby communicate the peace and blessing of the faith of the whole community in a representative way (see James 5:12ff). The service of Holy Communion may be right in many more cases than with those who are seriously ill. It is not the regular practice in nonconformist churches that perhaps it should be. There is much sharing of faith and worship of the whole community in the service which may be most helpful and full of healing for a sick person. I think it would help many of our people thus to receive communion.

## Prayer and healing the sick

There has been a service of 'Prayer for the visitation of the sick and the laying on of hands' of the Methodist Church. I imagine that like similar rites in other churches it needs updating. Combined with Holy Communion it should be a much more important part of the healing ministry of the Church. Because we eschew some of the showmanship associated with healing services, we should not opt out of our responsibility, as indicated in the New Testament, for our place in God's healing ministry. There ought to be a more thorough investigation in the churches of such prayer and healing. There are many cases when healing would be a natural outcome of prayer, as much as of other forms of treatment. As private healing practice is much more valid in a Christian community sense than public healing services, we ought to use it more.

Similarly confession and counselling ought to be a natural part of any community life, and nonconformist or non-catholic churches should get away from their prejudices against them.

## A final word must be with health

Wholeness and the full life of humanity is the aim for all people. This must be the reason for all our work and worship and prayer with people. We should therefore consider what a full life really is and what it contains of; rest, relaxation, sporting interests, relationships, exercise, prayer, quietness, study, service, and hard work. Although this is not the place to look at *life-styles* it is obvious that a simple and proper style of life for the Christian community today is very much involved in what we mean by health or wholeness.

## Questions for discussion

1. Discuss the meaning of health or wholeness as a biblical term.

2. What pastoral problems have you come up against that relate to sin, suffering or guilt?

3. How can psychiatry and counselling be used in co-operation with Christian community pastoral care?

4. Is there need now for a proper working out of visitation of prayer with, and healing of, the sick?

# 7 Death and Life

## Till death us do part

One of the saddest things in all pastoral work is the person left alone and rather incapable by the death of a partner. There is often an accompanying bitterness or instability which makes the whole situation so much worse. When it has been sudden or tragic, anguished questioning of faith and life goes on. There seemed no readiness for death, nor acceptance of its coming, and we have to be as helpful and sympathetic in these circumstances as we can. The lessons of being alone are not easy to learn, but perhaps we should try to learn these from people who have had to be alone most of their lives anyway. Changing the course of life to make us a little more independent, preparing for death and learning to face and accept it, are part of our own progress as pastors before we can help other people through their times of anguish.

No one will suggest that this is easy. You only have to ask yourself, 'How could I manage without ——', naming the person you value and love most, to realize what it involves. Hazlitt once wrote, 'No young man ever thinks he will die'. Older people may often think of death, but few are able to accept, the change that death brings in separation. The parting of the ways is so traumatic for some people that life ceases for a time to have meaning or value. There are questions of faith to trouble them. What really happens to the loved one? The involvement with the dead body, the physical mask of death, the problems of a certificate, the establishment of the will, the legal and business details, are sometimes overwhelming. Help in practical matters can of course be given.

## The loneliest time

Is there a pastoral pattern to be worked out in this 'life-force' situation which is different from the others in that it involves the facing of death? The pastor-visitor-friend, must have built up a right relationship over months and years to be helpful and effective now. It is a testing time for all that the Church and faith have meant. It is also a testing time for our previous teaching and preaching. I have often been amazed, perhaps quite wrongly, when people say things that show that they have never understood things of the faith that have been said over the years. We ought to deal far more with the subject of bereavement and death in teaching, so that people are not left unprepared and bereft of thought. The death and resurrection theme are tackled usually in the Lent to Good Friday period, and to some extent in Advent as well, but we should have a more extended preaching and teaching perhaps during the six weeks of the Easter season.

Some deaths within the community, and in most of our experiences, are tragic deaths. By that we mean that they occur suddenly, to people who are comparatively young and in circumstances of accident or misadventure. Sometimes the young person will have been suffering from an incurable disease. At times like these, there is every reason for people to be taken aback and to wonder where faith and love have gone. The caring of the pastoral community is very necessary then. No amount of previous teaching or 'preparation' will be able to ward off such a shock, but it may help people to come out constructively and without bitterness.

In death in the family, or with close friends, there is first the basic trauma of absence, held off a little by all the funeral arrangements. There is the stunning realization, as it comes home to the mind, that never again, in this life, will they see and have the loved person with them. Sometimes remorse and guilt are also involved. If only I had done that, if only they had not gone there, if only. . . . Helping people out of such guilt, which is often covered up or repressed, can be a pastoral problem, especially if it is not recognized. Much inner shock remains in the system of the person for a long time. According to their temperament and sensitivity, they may take two years or even up to five years, before there is anything like a return to living again.

We saw the need for prayer and blessing with the hands in the visiting of the sick. It is certainly true that in situations of death and sudden bereavement, spontaneous love has to be shown by the Christian visitor. The holding out of hands of love and care, literally, may help the person to cry, to respond, to share their grief. The affectionate embrace of a friend is probably more important than prayers, for most people, but prayer is also important when it brings people into the awareness of the presence of God. Prayer can help people to realize they are sharing God's own experience, that the Christian community upholds them, and that what is happening is still within the context of faith and not outside it.

## Preparation for age and retirement

We try to do a lot for young people, to prepare them for life. How much do we do for older people to prepare them for the remaining very different years, for the loss of loved ones, for becoming old, and for death? Perhaps we should have an ongoing house group, or interest group, such as the 'Council for the Elderly' or the 'Family Committee' to deal with these problems. We advocate conversation with and help for young people getting married, because of the effect upon home life this can have. What about the effect upon the life of a home of someone who is bereaved, or who is getting old, or is a sick and grieving person? It can help to break up a home and sometimes does.

West Indian and African homes in our experience prepare young people for the presence of death by having old people more a part of the family set-up and then by not being afraid to show them, literally, the face of death. People in the Western world are kept as far away from the body of death as possible and we try to sweep it all under the 'funeral director's' carpet. A lot of people later suffer because they have never been faced with death. Its appearance appals them and they cannot come to terms with this for their loved one.

Retirement and the limitations of old age also need preparation. It is astonishing how many people come to retire and find they have nothing to do and nowhere to turn. They make mistakes about going to live in a different place where they have no friends. They buy houses which they have dreamed about in their young days, but which they can now no longer cope with. Large gardens become a liability and the house itself, to which they gave so much care, can become a prison. Again a sympathetic visitor or a group of people meeting regularly, may help people to work out what is best and to be ready for the worst.

Age and sickness or geriatrics is not only a medical problem. More than ever there is stress on 'community care' and keeping people in their homes and flats and a well-known environment. Where people have their friends, it is usually a bad thing, unless absolutely necessary, to move them into an old peoples' home where they are 'limited' and wait for death. This is not to say of course that it is not a blessing to have good Homes available. If they are the sort of people who have been lonely and are increasingly isolated where they are, then a good Home with other people to converse with is much better.

Many more women than men are old-age problems for the community. In Notting Hill I reckoned it was a ratio of about twenty to one. The visitation of and the concern for these old people, is one of the priorities of pastoral care. Of course older people, like younger ones are all very different. Some are happy and joyous visits, that bring grace to you, others can be rather painful.

## The fear of death, and the life hereafter

Coming to terms with death is really coming to terms with time and the possibility of losing one's consciousness. That is difficult to comprehend and is perhaps one of the reasons why there is belief in the continuation of our personality. Another is of course the Christian teaching, about which more in a moment. It is not easy to assess how many people actually fear death. It would be useful if we could discuss all this with much more openness. It may be that some will feel it will be difficult and painful, instead of simple and natural. Their experience may have been of someone in great pain, although most people now do not face pain in death with modern drugs.

As Christians, our 'fear of death' is taken away because of our belief in life. Especially we believe in the life-power of Jesus, the one who has won the victory over death and evil and the grave. All of us will know or have heard stories of Christian people who have died with great faith and love and dignity and many without being afraid of death itself. (It is dignity in death, which most of us have the right to want to preserve.) We ought to examine what this means in practical terms. Does it mean that we shall not die? No, it does not mean that. Jesus did die. Does it mean that all are immortal? No, we do not believe, in spite of a lot of misunderstanding, in the 'immortality of the soul' (i.e. the going on for ever of each person whatever happens). We believe that it is natural for the soul (the person) to die (as opposed to Greek thought), and that only in Christ shall all be made alive. It is the relationship to Jesus that makes for real and new life.

The question of how, and in what form, we cannot answer. We only go so far as to say that personality lives (the resurrection of the body), if that person is linked in love to God through Christ. To those who have had no chance of finding this in Christianity, we believe that God makes it possible for the principle of Christ to come home to all his people. Scientifically one could show, according to one's viewpoint, the probability or improbability of life form after death. Astronomically one could explore the possibilities of super-space and extra-terrestrial spheres, from black holes to reverse universes. Christianly, humanly, what is required is a word of truth and a word of love. We cannot know what will happen to us, that is quite beyond human experience. We have, however, a strong trust in love as we have seen and known it in Jesus and found it reflected in human relationships. If Jesus says, 'There is a place for you', that is space for life, for all who trust the way of love as the way of victory, then personally I trust that word and am satisfied.

The Cross in human life is often associated with all the problems and pains of growing old and the limitations of life. The pain and burden to be carried is really a false symbol of the Christian life. We are not looking at a crucifix but an empty cross, which is for us, in Jesus, the way of victory. If we can take the limitations of old age, and the oncoming of death and make of them but an open way to new experiences of life and resurrection, we shall have helped people as well as ourselves. We can show what is true and how the challenge of our experience to live fully, is the way Jesus went, beyond the limitations put upon him, to the joy of the morning.

### Arranging the funeral

Our knowledge of practical details can help in a difficult time.

(a) Be practical. This can mean advising on undertakers, and advising that an itemized estimate of costs should be asked for. You may not feel like checking charges, or the bereaved may not, but this often saves expense. Religious services (some fees may be payable) should be arranged with the clergyman and the facts given to the undertaker. Death grants are payable to most people and should be applied for with a death certificate. Insurance policies, etc., also require death certificates and these may be obtained from the Registrar of Deaths, where the death should have been registered as soon as possible.

The National Citizens' Advice Bureaux Council have published a four-page leaflet, 'Practical Problems following the Death of a Relative or Friend'. A doctor's signed form is required for a cremation.

Time and effort so spent is an important pastoral job, and should not be forgotten.

(b) The funeral service should contain as much of the request of the bereaved family as is possible to our theology and aesthetic feeling. Usually a great deal is left to the minister, and the kind of understanding and sympathy he puts into conducting the service can mean a great deal for the people involved. An English service will on the whole not be a long one but services arranged by someone from any other part of the world can be long. They can also be very real celebrations of the faith. We should never be impatient, but give all the time and attention we can to the funeral service which speaks of the cultural as well as religious background of the family and which is deliberately given a great deal of time and signifiance. If we are not geared to this because of our English background, then we must realize and learn that the healthy acceptance and rejoicing as well as the deep sorrow expressed in such a service does a great deal to prepare people to find emotional relief. This can otherwise be pent up in inhibited people and can cause sickness and trouble later on.

(c) We may be asked our advice on cremation, and will need to indicate that the faith we have does not include a requirement that molecular, bodily recomposition must take place, which some people still feel is necessary. We need also to combat various forms of 'spiritism' which believe that you have trouble in some way with the spirit of the person departed. This is not just with 'unsophisticated' people, but arises in all sorts of people in peculiar ways. Especially we shall want to say, that whether or not spirits exist in some form, they have no terror for the Christian.

(d) Preparation for the funeral and all that is associated with bereavement in a home is another of the life-force situations. Once again there is a challenge to our pastoral care in these ways:

i. There is a need for friendship and help, which can bring a great new dimension for some families and which can display the love of God and the care of the Christian community as nothing else could.

ii. There is what you say and pray in the home. Wherever possible I go to the home to come with the family to the service, especially when there is not a cemetery chapel. It is very helpful for members of the Christian community to be able to do this too, expressing the community's concern. It is often possible to pray there and to bring home to otherwise non-Christian relatives something of the meaning of the love and mercy of God.

iii. Prayers and addresses at the service can be important for preaching the Good News. I don't mean a long sermon, but there are some valid 'evangelical' occasions in such a service.

iv. There is care required in the following days and weeks. In my experience, the worst time for people is around six months after the death. A lot of love and attention is required then.

## New life and resurrection

(a) First let us look at the Christian life as one of growing maturity. Faith in Christ and wholeness or salvation involve a point where we could say we pass from death to life, but the Christian life is also a life of growing and discovering. Growing old gracefully is something for all to aim at. Perhaps we should start an Old Age Anonymous! So it is that sanctification or growth in holiness, or the discovery of peace in the individual or the community, all have something to say about the end product of the life of faith. Wholeness in this sense does not mean the ability to be active and to do a lot of things, rather, the ability in faith, to rest in the goodness of God and declare it in our lives.

(b) The experience of conversion is not just a change of heart for the teen-ager, it is a possible new experience of life more abundant for everyone at any age, especially perhaps when the closeness in thought and experience of death and life is realized. The Lazarus story of the Gospel of John, and Saul Kane's experience in 'The Everlasting Mercy' are perhaps apt illustrations of 'conversion-resurrection'. We have a lot to learn about resurrection and new life experienced here and now (cf. John 11).

(c) Resurrection as an experience. Whatever we believe, we cannot know the new form of new life. The 'spiritual body' of Paul (1 Corinthians 15) cannot be speculated about with any profit. The Christian community however needs to think more about the new life which begins now, in recognizable forms. It is indeed our experience of resurrection now that enables us to understand and believe in the resurrection then. It was the presence of the living Christ with the disciples that enabled them to understand and believe and preach the Resurrection as the central matter of the Christian Gospel. The presence of the Living Christ with us, in Christian community (the Body of Christ) at the Eucharist (the Body of Christ), in the world around us and in other people, is part of true Christian experience.

Jesus often told his disciples to look around them to see what God was doing. He took from nature and the everyday world the things that spoke of and indicated that his Father was at work and was dynamically present. We need to do this for the theme of resurrection and new life.

One of the truths of the faith that has come home to me strongly in the community in Notting Hill, especially in association with wonderful Easter worship experiences and the real and powerful sense of the Easter message made manifest in our own lives, is the reality of resurrection. Resurrection in the lives of those given new hope, new accommodation, new jobs, new possibilities; resurrection in human relationships, in people made new, in love shown between people, actually happens. There is resurrection in the change made by organizations working in the community with people. There is resurrection in the understanding people have of God coming among them, of his presence on the streets and in the homes where love and faith have taken the place of strife and bitterness and prejudice.

A Theology of Hope for our day will take into account this new dimension of resurrection in daily life. For this also we need the expectation and challenge of life that comes by death.

## Questions for discussion

1. Have you ever experienced new love and life through personal tragedy?

2. How can we prepare for retirement?

3. Do you fear death, and do you look for new life, now and hereafter?

4. Why is resurrection an important part of the good news, from the first days until now? (Read relevant passages in 1 Corinthians 15, etc., in 1 Thessalonians 4 and 5 and in Colossians 1 and 3.)

# 8 Building Up Christian Community

## What kind of response are we looking for in evangelism?

We noted in chapter 4 that commitment is supposedly made reluctantly in some aspects of life today. We saw that what was probably required within the Christian community was such demonstration of love and sacrifice that the way of Jesus was made plain. The way of Jesus is often shown best by the community as a whole living his life. The preaching of the word in the church is only part of that proclamation. If there is bitterness and strife or the demonstration of all the bad things that society has in plenty, there is not much chance that a converting word can be preached in that situation. Where there is an atmosphere of trust and a community of care, what is felt and seen may with confidence be told and responded to.

The young Christian or the older person who is drawn into community will not be able to make a mature response of all that a theology of the Christ can mean. That requires a life-time of relationship. The response should, and more naturally can be, an awareness that Jesus means something to them. It represents a direction of life and a belonging to a community. It is in Christian community that a 'Jesus-image' is found and the community is therefore the greatest means of evangelism that we can have.

The sacrament of Baptism should be administered regularly to give opportunity within the community for participating in renewal of vows and discovering its meaning. The sacrament of Confirmation, similarly, should be administered regularly, as at the great Festivals of Advent, Easter and Whitsun, so that its converting and challenging power may be widely spread. Confirmation is a reaching out to all who will come that way, as a stage in Christian development, even if, after it, people do not necessarily reach the standard of commitment that is expected sometimes in Church membership. Our pastoral drive at confirming people, is not to evangelize in the sense of increasing numbers, but to make available the opportunities and the mercies of God, which is what real evangelism is about.

The building up of community is a matter of faith as much as of numbers. This does not mean that numbers are not important. I feel that there needs to be a Christian community of over 100 and probably 200 people to demonstrate effectively by its life the range of ministry. It is when community is being built up in this way, that it can then appeal to further people by its life. There seems to be an area of about 100–150 in membership, when a kind of effective bursting through in faith and life can be achieved. This is perhaps a social as well as a spiritual phenomenon, which we do not realize sufficiently. The fact that the majority of our church communities are under this number, may be one of the reasons why real growth does not take place. It may seem to be a vicious circle, but it could also mean that we have to concentrate on properly spaced centres of growth in order to achieve this. It does not mean that the many missionary areas of towns and cities have to be abandoned, however, because in them we have a great commission. We cannot opt out of this task of compassion and love. Nor can we neglect the lessons that are being learned in such situations about the Gospel and its insights for today.

### Leadership

One thing we must give attention to is a theology of leadership. Leadership, in middle-class concepts, refers to ability to speak and lead a meeting or group. In the Church it also has to do with experience, spiritual or otherwise, which is recognizable and which the person is able to communicate in an articulate way. The preacher and teacher and the one who can organize other people is therefore a leader.

Other forms of leadership are in 'upper-class' society, hereditarily received and naturally assumed without question. In 'working-class' situations it is thrust upon people in emergencies and never thought about until something requires to be done. There is also the leadership which comes from groups of people responding and moving together in particular ways. A murmur can become a roar without an apparent lead being given, but it depends on a kind of cultic similarity or basic feeling for a course of action. We do well to study these and other forms in more depth within church life. This is especially important in areas where we say there is little leadership. We mean by that that there is no leadership of the recognizable kind, which will stand up and speak out. The inner city areas or other failing situations for the church are beginning to realize that as long as leadership is imported from elsewhere, or continues to be carried on by people who have moved out of the geographical area but come back to keep the work going, there can be no emergence of indigenous leadership. We should take risks in giving unlikely people and apparently unqualified people jobs within the life of the church. It is painful to see old people carrying on year after year while young people are there for a time and then leave. Young people, perhaps younger and more immature than some regulations allow for, must be given the chance to do things in their way. People who seem to have no gifts in doing things in the institutional church manner and ethos, should be allowed to discover other gifts to do things in non-traditional ways. Our structures must be flexible enough to have things done differently in different places, to suit the area and the people and the local situation. An imposed pattern of church life for every place is a sociological nonsense. It is one of the reasons why the building up of communities in some places never seems to be achieved. Leadership and new forms of church life are required if we are to see a growing and the development that comes from such growing.

It is not to denigrate middle-class leadership which revolves around education and ability, to say that we need to explore other ways of using people in leadership than the formal ways. It may be that the end result is to have more people who are speaking and leading groups or preaching or teaching and that would not be a bad thing! To leave ways of opening up participation unexplored, is to prevent many people from entering into the life and work of the church, which is at present basically a middle-class society.

One way of enabling people to participate is in Community Leadership. This is not the same as the position of Class Leader. In the first place it relates to the Community Roll and seeks to care for all the people there. It enables people to relate to others in a particular group of families given to them. This can be in a geographical area, or it can be by trade or profession or those with similar concerns. No specific brief on what and how this should be done needs to be given. The leaders are asked to relate to people in any way they can, which means that there are several different possibilities. They could become resource people who give advice and to whom people will turn. It could mean that they deliver newsletters and other material. It may mean that they invite people to their home for a group or house church, which they themselves may or may not lead. It could mean that they start a specific project in a certain street, or within the community at large, asking those in their care to help them in varying ways. Guidance can be given regularly to leaders of this kind and gathering them together from time to time is obviously important so that they can discuss what they are doing and learn from one another. The free hand given to them in pursuing their work within the Christian community can mean new things breaking out and a building up process that comes from learning and discovering.

Another way for people to discover their leadership is in worship. We should note that Church of God congregations, for instance, encourage all their people, from an early age, to take part in testimony and singing. They may start with one line, or one verse, in ways reminiscent of the Christian Endeavour groups. We should not keep so regularly to form in worship that we prevent such movements of the spirit and such freedom of participation. People grow as they take part and commit themselves as they feel that they belong.

In Notting Hill there have been for a long time teams of people taking part in worship, enabling small participation that leads on to greater. The position of Worship Leader may or may not lead on to the position of Lay (or Local) Preacher, but it is an important role that should be recognized within the church. Free parts of the worship in which people can share, or where the concerns of the community are freely expressed, should perhaps be a regular feature of all worship. There is a sense in which every act of worship should contain aspects of liturgy or order and form and others of spontaneity. Free orders of worship, that literally happen on the spot, may be disturbing for some, but they enable a more general participation which may in turn produce new leadership.

Not that leadership always needs to be noticeable. There are many members of Christian community whom I have known who play a very effective part in the life of the community by being what they are, where they are. Their quiet faith expressed in their daily lives is often more able to lead people to God than many other ways of leadership.

One other matter of leadership needs to be mentioned. This is that leadership will be exercised by different people at different times. Not only should this be on a kind of 'rota basis' for meetings and worship but the natural abilities and expertise that people have will mean that whereas one person is acknowledged on a certain subject, someone else will naturally take over at another session on another subject. This is a Team concept of leadership, which means that in Team ministry, for example, some people represent the Team of the Church and its leadership in pastoral affairs, while another group will be the authority in social work, in worship or in international affairs.

In all these ways we acknowledge that leadership is a very diverse thing. It can be exercised in a number of ways by very different people. It is a theological and biblical issue that the gifts of leadership are bestowed on everyone and it is our responsibility to see that all the gifts and charisma are used. They should be explored and expoited and fully realized within each person as well as in the whole community.

### Liturgy

We have spoken of life-force situations in the individual and how these are reflected in the life and ministry, death and resurrection of Jesus. In a Christian community, this is emphasized and high-lighted by the celebration of the Christian Year. It is an experience, to which I can testify, that the communities that really follow the Christian Year and its enactment of the whole Gospel of Jesus harness the natural rhythm of the year to the Gospel and the building up of its people in faith and life.

Beginning at Advent, there is the theme of Judgement and Crisis and of course the doctrine of the Incarnation. Here the coming and birth of Jesus is seen as part of the plan of God and of his natural way of coming into the world amongst people. This of course is followed by Christmas, Epiphany or the manifestation, demonstration, or light-bringing to the world. Lent and Holy Week to Easter, the Easter season of five weeks, the Pentecostal theme of the Church and the world and latter-Trinity with its missionary emphases, are all supremely significant for the Christian community. Where there is the reading of the Bible and its study and preaching from the lectionary and festival worship that goes with these, the community knows itself to be acting out the life and ministry of Jesus in the world. It is a great building up process that goes on year after year. During that time, the special seasons relate to calling to discipleship (as in Lent and Easter) and confirmation in church membership as at Advent, Easter and Whitsun. Where the process is followed with care and attention, people are drawn to the marvellous life story which becomes their own.

Liturgy is basically a piece of public service, which is much more than worship. It is worship plus the relationship to life, intercession for life and response to the word of God in life. The ordering of the liturgy therefore is part of the building-up process of Christian community. It is true of course that all the people are not there all the time, but as they are drawn into its power and meaning they become more and more zealous at being there and being part of the process. Whereas, in Notting Hill, our Easters used to be the times when people from other parts of the world came to festival worship and English people went on holiday, they soon became the occasions that people did not want to miss, and English people put off their holiday or days off, until after Easter worship. This is only an example of the drawing power of the Gospel as proclaimed in the liturgy.

When people are also able, through the careful Christian education of the community, to associate their life-force situations with those of the life of Jesus, the Gospel comes home with powerful impact. I know of a young married couple who, to get to Easter morning Vigil at 5.0 a.m., 'While it was still dark', ran, like Peter and John, to the tomb dark church, to wait outside for the knocking and entry to the light of Easter morning. I know of families in Notting Hill, who worshipped on Easter morning with a real and deep sense of resurrection, because they had been re-housed by a Housing Trust and gave thanks and praise for the new life which had come to them.

## Making members

There should be a much more natural and systematic approach to making members and bringing people to confirmation. Some of the ways of doing this are as follows:

i. A membership class should be constantly running in the Christian community. Apart from the break in the summer time for holidays, the class can run from September to Advent, from New Year to Easter, or from Lent to Whitsun. If it is established that the Confirmation class is there all the time, it becomes one of the weekly meetings of the church, with much more validity than many. It should have prior claim not only on the presbyters time, but on the time of a rota of people who share in its leadership and make their own contributions to its teaching and learning.

ii. The scheme of lessons, or sessions, needs to be worked out with imagination. There is a natural four-part grouping of sessions; the devotional life (prayer, bible reading, worship, etc.); the doctrines of the faith (perhaps based on the creed); the life of the Church and the daily life of the Christian. The imagination comes in when the people are, for instance, taken on a tour of the church and look at all the furnishings and aspects of the building. They can themselves prepare and share in an act of worship. They can talk about or write up their impressions of a Communion service. They could attend a Church Council meeting or a meeting of one of the church committees to see all that goes on. They could be addressed by the Church Treasurer, by a Church Steward or Communion Steward or Community leader, etc.

iii. The approach to people for membership is best done by careful attention to the Community Roll. The family committee or a pastoral group should, every year, go through the Community Roll and make a list of the people to be asked to consider membership. At the same time, in Church, during a discipleship service in Lent, or at the Church birthday at Whitsun, an appeal to membership and the following of Jesus Christ can be made.

With all the opportunities that a live Christian community provides there should be no lack of candidates for membership in the Church. The building up of the community depends on the life and love of that community, for others to join and to be built up in the faith.

### Questions for discussion

1. Consider again what we are asking people to do in responding to Christ and his Church. What will it mean to them?

2. Study 1 Corinthians 13 and Ephesians 2 and 3 as descriptions of the building up of Christian community.

3. Explore the possibility of new forms of leadership within the Church.

4. Is your church using the liturgical movement of the Christian year as a way of building up its people in faith?

# 9 Pastoral Evangelism

## Motives, methods and meaning

If pastoral care, or its urban equivalent, is to do with
caring for people, meeting with them for their own sakes
and as part of our responsibility as a Christian community,
where does evangelism come in? Some people would feel
emphatically that, in most cases, it does not. Others would
feel that as the end of all our work is winning people for
Christ, then all our visiting and relationship with people
is ultimately for this purpose. Let us examine carefully
our motives, methods and meaning.

There is a real sense in which our meeting with people
and care for them is in itself an act of Jesus, and needs
to be no more explicit than that. Yet we know that all our
relationships with people will bring us at some point to
the question of motivation and to the aim of our enter-
prise. We should not draw back from the fact that we are
here for the purpose of bringing people into relationship
with Jesus Christ and therefore with his Body, the Christian community. Many of us would be content, as far as
methods are concerned, to leave it there. When we have
said 'Come and see', we leave Jesus to make his own impression and impact. There are always occasions, however,
when we are Jesus Christ to other people. What they see
of us, will be all that they see of him. This is of course a
terrible responsibility. It means that they will ask us
questions either openly in terms of what our beliefs and
motives are, or by way of seeing us and observing how we
act and love. If our actions answer their questions to their
satisfaction, their response may then be towards Jesus
Christ and discipleship.

If, in fact, our methods of 'evangelism' involve constant
harassment of people, in their homes and in their minds

and lives, we may do the opposite of what we want and drive them far from Christianity. Our care really must not have strings attached any more than Jesus' healing work was done in order to attract followers. Jesus healed because he loved and cared for people in their need. If they then wanted to be disciples he was at pains to point out what it would involve in terms of hardship and discipline and ultimately the cross. Our caring ministry and the work of pastoral care, taking into account the 'cure' of the whole person, will be happily fulfilled if people are brought to new possibilities of a full life and relieved of so many things that oppressed them previously. In that position of freedom, if they then want to ask. 'What do we do and how can we do it?' we can then take up the whole matter of what is involved in being a follower of Jesus Christ. These opportunities do occur, but we must not confuse a loving outgoing concern and care with what we hope to achieve by doing it—this, even when we believe fundamentally that fullness of life in the end depends on a response to Jesus.

It is a pity that within the faith of the Church, we cannot hold together caring service and evangelism. They are part of the whole and we need to harness the concern of the two approaches to the question of mission. We must not shrug off the other aspect of mission because our own emphasis happens to be different. In the end, they belong together.

## A scheme of pastoral care which involves mission

I outline here a scheme which has been built up over the years in Notting Hill. There is nothing outstanding about it, but it has worked well.

(a) It came into being after experiments with *Church Neighbourhood Councils* and geographical schemes with church people and others working together. In these a minister and other leaders bring together any number of caring people. The main problem we found was their relationship to each other, in that they lacked real co-ordination. They were in contact with all kinds of people but we had to begin with working out their own relationships rather than the needs of other people in the areas concerned.

(b) The eventual scheme starts with the assumption that all people in association with the Christian community are our concern and responsibility. This usually means the Community Roll of the church. This should be as comprehensive as possible, rather than making limits on who is included. It will include the families of baptized children, the children and families of those in Junior Church and clubs and other organizations. There will be those people still in the area who were married at the church and adherents as well as members. Some will be those referred to us out of social-community care, where it is appropriate that they be included on a church list. Others will be the kind of contacts that are always being made by our people, who bring, or mention, a family, a friend, a need, an interest and the like. On the understanding that all these people are just as important and just as much our responsibility as are the members of the Church, we then have to organize our care in a rather different way from that of most other lists of communicant members.

(c) The scheme will involve Community Leaders and Co-ordinators or similar names to describe the same thing. It is hard to find a better name for the office or work or occupation than *Community Leader*. (Class Leader is obviously out of date, and related in the past only to those who 'belonged'). In Notting Hill there are about eighty Community Leaders and additional numbers where couples act together. They are each responsible for about six families, usually in the immediate area where they live. The kind of relationship which is built up with the families depends on literature distribution (newsletters, community letters, Festival and seasonal cards, membership tickets where appropriate, baptismal certificates, stewardship material, etc.), on occasional house groups or meals together, on area action and projects, on visiting, especially where people are ill or in need. The Community Leader will be the 'address' or the 'person' to which people come when help is required. They will all see and do their job in different ways according to their personality and ability and weaknesses.

*Co-ordinators* (there have been many searches for a better word) are the people in charge of the twelve main areas of work. They will usually have some social or pastoral-care work qualification or gift. They will be leaders in the community in every way. They are each responsible for about six Community Leaders within the area of their co-ordination. They take special responsibility for the Leaders themselves, although they also take first action in any problem or difficult case that the Community Leader brings.

(d) *The Pastoral Council* is formed of the Co-ordinators, Ministers, and any other sectional leaders such as those for Youth, the Elderly, etc. This will meet about four times a year and is responsible for a wide spectrum of work related to the well-being of the whole community. Such matters include: counselling, special visitation, re-treats, meals, good neighbour schemes, holidays, newsletters, pastoral theology courses, training session and conferences of various kinds, understanding leadership, hospitality and service and membership. Within the new Methodist structures this could be done by the work of the Family Committee plus its special Pastoral Committee together with what is intended by the Neighbourhood Committee.

If within the structures all the Community Leaders cannot be brought to the Church Council, it is worth having meetings from time to time involving all of them.

I envisage this scheme working out as it stands, in most city/urban areas where churches work together and have one Church Council and administrative base. In the usual urban Methodist Circuit there is no reason why the whole of the Circuit's pastoral care should not be organized in one such overall scheme.

## How is mission involved?

(a) First of all the value of such a scheme is as a network of communication. In areas where it is difficult to keep contact with people, it is all the more important that a communications net should be continually thrown out to catch and find and hold and help. Information will go out to the various people through the network and most important 'notices' can reach all the people within a week of passing them on to the Co-ordinators. Contact, encouragement and witness pass on at the same time. Back from the people come various concerns, needs, calls for action by members of staff and the rest.

(b) As an 'evangelical exercise', the case is obvious. It will depend in part on the kind of activity and attitudes of the various community leaders. It has the effect, however, of constantly reminding, stimulating and calling people to church worship and to service. Many other people are drawn in by the individual families passing on the word or making the introduction.

(c) Projects or ongoing activities will include house groups, outings, visiting campaigns, street Sunday schools, meals, cleaning and decorating, play programmes, summer activities, holidays, local community efforts. They will be arranged and organized where necessary by the whole Council or by Area Co-ordinators, with the people. We must all the time keep in mind the cardinal principle of community development or working *with* people rather than for them. All these things have both a caring and a winning aspect bound up together and all embrace and enhance the meaning and value of Christian community. They also mean that different things can go on in different areas and ideas thrown up in one locality can be tried in others.

(d) Community leaders deal with the members among their families no differently from any others, accept that the Annual Membership tickets are given out through the Co-ordinators to the Community Leaders on Covenant Sunday in a special act of membership dedication. The careful working through of the Community Roll needs to be done each year to produce a constant flow of candidates for membership/confirmation classes.

(e) One Christian research student once challenged a statement of mine in an article. It was that the properly organized, caring, community-concerned church, far from taking away from the emphasis on growth in membership added to it. I set down for her in statistics the growth of the Notting Hill community which has always been orientated towards the wider community and its needs. I think they prove the point I am making about the pastoral system and its evangelical significance.

The Church membership increased from about 80 in 1960 to 370 or so at the end of the 1960s. It has kept at that level in spite of the demolition of property in the immediate area and the moving away of large numbers of the population ever since. Now that the new development is bringing people back, a new increase is expected. During the same period the Community Roll has grown from 200 to 2,000 and there are in the pastoral scheme alone some 100 leaders. It is true of course that the increase was partly accounted for at one period by the large number of people from other countries joining the fellowship, community and membership of the Church. This was due to (i) the care and loving openness of the Christian community as a whole that concerned itself about housing, jobs, children and health; (ii) a worshipping community that was not set in particular ways of worship and life but changed and renewed itself as it went along with all the contributions that other peoples had to make; (iii) a carefully organized pastoral system as described above that kept in touch and brought people closer to the Church and to Jesus.

## Organization essential

In the essential and only really valid evangelism of the Christian Community itself, these things must be held together. A life-style and a worship style that is renewed and continually renewable is vital. However well organized you are, nothing will be achieved if there is no loving, caring community with which people can relate. On the other hand a great deal of love and helpful worship and community spirit will drift into nothing if the gift of the Holy Spirit in administration is not exercsed and fully used. A properly run and efficiently organized system of pastoral care is essential for any community to grow. I have always felt that what is lacking in so much church life, and means that we struggle and fail and decline, is hard work and careful administration. Do we leave that efficiency at the office or boardroom or factory floor or school when we come to church? Is there something un-holy about doing things with real management efficiency and with meticulous care to detail? I think that the holi-ness of the gift of the Holy Spirit in administration gives the lie to such a view. Without that particular gift of Pentecost many churches and communities founder and fail. It goes without saying that it depends upon a wide and full ministry of the whole church to make it possible. If you leave it to the ordained presbyters little can be achieved! If I can labour the point, it means that there must be a Secretary who can give some considerable time to the operation of the scheme. The overall care of at least one of the presbyters on the staff is essential. The production of revised community lists twice a year is very demanding, but very necessary. The system of getting names and addresses on to the Community Roll has to be looked at carefully. One way is to have a 'New names and addresses' book, which is always around, brought to every meeting and kept easily accessible to people. It needs writing up each week after the busy opportunity of Sunday. It requires opportunities after each service of worship or community gathering to be used and checked and changed. Do you provide an opportunity after each service for instance (over coffee and/or conversation period) when the names and addresses of new people or people who have moved can be put down as a vitally important part of the life of a caring community?

The other job of good personnel management and administration is to see that as many people as possible are put into active service and participation in councils, projects and action groups for the Church and the wider community.

Who says that real community care is not basic evangelism!

**Questions for discussion**

1. What is evangelism? How is it best exercised within Christian community?

2. Check up on your own church pastoral scheme. Does it need changing and improving? In what ways?

3. Look up the passages in Ephesians and Corinthians that describe the gifts of leadership within the Christian community. Are they all being exercised in your community?

4. Is it right to 'make members' today? What process does our church follow to do this? What can we do to help?

## 10  The Devotional Life of the Christian Community

**Spirituality**
This word describes a variety of practices, attitudes, devotional exercises and life-styles and has different connotations for different people. Yet, to talk about the devotional life of a Christian community we have to look at the wider context, because so much happens within the community that needs to be related to its 'devotional life'. Sometimes the idea of spirituality gets diverted into areas of personal devotion and exercise, which taken in isolation cannot describe the essential meaning. While individuals certainly have a devotional life of their own, true spirituality can only be attained in a Christian community.

So today, within church life, and outside it, groups, community houses, extended family groupings, retreat houses, centres of renewal, all show the upsurge of desire for and need of a true spirituality. Community houses as begun in Notting Hill and many other places, Ashram Communities like that in Sheffield, and many other attempts at community in the Spirit of Jesus, have all related spirituality to life and have sought a new life-style as part of their endeavour.

The caring ministry of the Church in its support for people has to be aware of the need for renewed spirituality within the life of the Church and the individual.

**Where does the ordinary church community find its spirituality?**
Some of the community will be involved in group living, in house groups or discussion and prayer groups, in Taizé and renewal groups of different kinds. There should always

be an encouragement by the whole Church to such group-ings within the total life. Some people will explore the riches of other denominations and other religions and again they should have the community's support. We found many attempts at and many opportunities for this participation at the Notting Hill Ecumenical Centre, in the Sion Catholic Convent and on the Portobello Road generally: Sufi, Divine Light, Hari Krishna and Ecumeni-cal Christian exploration always gave opportunity for discovery in other people's spirituality.

These will always be for the minority of our Christian community. Though an early morning Communion service (and every sizeable Christian community should have such weekly) is a great experience in fellowship, it is not the Communion of whole Community and cannot therefore speak of the Community's total devotional life. An essential part of spirituality therefore for all Christians is the communal act of family worship, whatever form it takes. This is where the individuals and families and various groupings can come together to share, to contri-bute, to participate and to receive from one another. This is where we need to give so much more attention to wor-ship, so that it comes alive, and people make the great discoveries of the life in the Spirit, where all renewal starts. I am not often blessed with the 'beatific vision', or other great spiritual experiences, alone; I can often find the presence of Jesus in the Body of Christ, when I wor-ship in a real community. The Body is truly that company of people who represent and re-form him, today. The emphasis on Holy Communion, and all that it means in terms of taking, blessing, breaking, sharing and sending has been mentioned earlier. The concept of the Body in the Eucharist is the dynamic emphasis on the spirituality of the common life.

In the common life, spirituality may be very different for each one of us, but because it is a communal spiritual-ity, it is complimentary. What I lack in one or more aspects of spirituality, is made up for and provided by someone else. Here again we see the significance of a really mixed community, with all the different contributions and insights it has to offer.

## Prayer and life

A debate must go on all the time, as to how far spirituality is worked out in prayer and devotional exercises and how far it is part of the working out of everyday life. The 'prayer is work' theme of activists among us is balanced in true community by prayer as a spiritual exercise which 'stands back' in relief from everyday life and pressures. The ideas of the life of prayer and prayer being life, are brought together in Christian community, as they have been in monastic and other communities for centuries. The people who prayed together, worked together and in livelihood and faith depended on each other. When spirituality is so described, then there is less likelihood of a dichotomy between prayer and life.

Is there a communal way of relating prayer and life for the normal Christian community? I see more point in attempting to seek for a communal way or rule than an individualistic one. One has assumed, often mistakenly, that 'communities', monasteries, priories and the like are all right for those who want to get away from it all. Where monks and nuns and religious of the past have tried to be world-denying, rather than world-embracing, they have actually denied the faith with an ascetic heresy. This is acknowledged by many writers on the theme today, in the Religious Orders (cf. Sister Madeline in *Solitary Refinement*—SCM Press). But the local Christian community should find it possible to look at its life together, as the context in which a personal spirituality can be worked out and lived. In the course of the last few years, I shared in the attempt to do this in Notting Hill, where we tried to find communal disciplines in some aspects of our life.

## Let us start with the Bible

The production of our own lectionary in 1963 stemmed from our belief that in the middle of city life we should examine the Bible together, draw theological insight from it, and find spiritual inspiration. I find real strength as an individual in reading the Bible daily, partly because I know that the community as a whole is engaged in it and is thinking about the morning sermon to be preached from the lectionary. In times of despondency I have been discouraged by wondering how many actually do! I strongly believe however in the centrality of Bible reading and study, guided by all the aids, commentaries, translations that are at our disposal. The great significance of a lectionary is this communal thought, discipline and education in spirituality. I don't believe that Christians can exist in community without the 'Jesus Book'. It is fundamental to Christian spirituality. The present lectionary which we follow is that of the Joint Liturgical Group (*now* in the *Methodist Service Book*) representing all the churches and used throughout the churches. It is a two-year cycle of working through the Bible with the great themes and sequences of the Christian year, the life and ministry of Christ and the ongoing life of the Church.

## What about a prayer lectionary?

To be more precise in the use of words, we are talking about a daily pattern of prayer subjects or themes used communally as a lectionary is. We have from time to time in Notting Hill (and it is something that I would advocate experiments with elsewhere) tried to produce a corporate plan for prayers for the day. This was not an office, which most people would find difficult to maintain, but a suggested outline for everyone to share. The system is that the community should use different days of the week, to emphasize different aspects of prayer life, so that you had a weekly rhythm of prayer to go with a monthly rhythm of worship and a yearly rhythm of the Christian year.

Monday would be the day to remember praise, for example, Tuesday would be for meditation, Wednesday for confession, Thursday for thanksgiving, Friday for intercession and Saturday for petition. The idea is not to have set times, which could not work for everyone, but rather that, at any time of day, when the opportunity presented itself, people can join, if only briefly, in the ongoing prayer on that day. It is surprising, when you start thinking in this way, how many chances there are to bring, say, thanksgiving or confession to the fore as you are occupied, or travelling by bus, or seeing a tree in bloom, or looking at the advertisements up an escalator!

## Team community rule

We came to Notting Hill as a team, with the idea of establishing a rule or discipline of some kind, first of team life, then more generally. We had prayers together each morning of the week, some of which are still extant. Scarcely ever was it possible for any others than the ministerial team to be there. Sometimes wives and families joined in, but it became too much of an 'in thing', with just the parsons involved, as any other small group rule of life would be. We felt that the emphasis needed to be moved to the whole community and to Sunday mornings, to be a valid spirituality. The orders of worship that are produced throughout the Christian year have this in mind. The 'daily office' becomes for most people a weekly one. The life and rule of the team becomes more peripheral, like that of any other group within the community, and not central to it. I do not feel, now, that any form of worship or prayer discipline is relevant in the modern world which does not concern, and seek to include, most of our people. I cannot find the idea of parsons or closed orders saying prayers on our behalf a satisfactory concept, or valid as real intercession, although I do not of course quarrel with those who do. This is not because I do not see the validity of intercessory prayer but because it implies that the rest of us are engaged in the 'wicked world' and are not praying, or cannot pray, in all that we do and are.

## Devotion in an activist community

Most people in active Christian communities find it difficult, for one reason or another, to set aside the same time every day for a period of quietness, or deliberate prayer, using some daily office. I feel that we should not be anxious about this and about our 'failures' in devotional patterns. Spirituality is not contrived and the important thing is to take opportunities when they arrive and to build up a spirituality that relates to others and is a valid part of life. I see this sort of spirituality as being a balance between awareness and relaxation. The discipline of awareness is to be found in what you do with your life in relation to other people as much as to yourself. For instance, it is as important to be on time, and not to keep other people waiting, as it is to say your prayers at a certain time. Ordinary daily discipline towards others is surely spirituality. Relaxation for some will be in gardening or walking or playing or watching football. They can be 'spiritual' exercises if they enable people to relax and find a more whole and balanced life.

To advocate that prayer is work is only to say that there should not be a false barrier between the sacred and the secular. It is worth reading Douglas Rhymes' little book called *Prayer in the Secular City*, where all life is seen as a vehicle of the holy. As with Jesus, the natural, human, 'secular' world can show us the holy and God at work. In my experience there is an essential truth in St Bernard's assertion that he was no less at prayer when washing up in the monastery kitchen than when on his knees in the chapel. I have a conviction which arises from a great deal of experience of cleaning out church lavatories, that every candidate for the ministry should be tested on his or her ability to clean out lavatories as much as on what sort of devotional life he or she has. This is not 'mere activism', it is a matter of an attitude of mind. A person who cannot clean out, properly, a dirty lavatory, or do some similar work, has not the right attitude to God or people. It is also saying a deeply theological thing that spirituality is world embracing and not world denying. The God who becomes flesh, incarnate in Jesus, has come into ordinary human life. Our spirituality has to be found there also. In community, a way of observing and celebrating this kind of spirituality is to have what we have called 'fun days', which means a party of people enjoying themselves together as they clean out the church, or a street or yard, or an old person's home for decorating.

Prayer is therefore the way the Christian lives his life in community. This active and dynamic approach is not a denial of the need for prayer. It is exemplified in the various aspects of prayer seen in the context of community. For example, Adoration, which is 'to pray out', is getting outside yourself to others and to God. Process Theology speaks of God as 'becoming', as part of his dynamic relationship with the world. Prayer that is also 'becoming', emphasizes that dynamic relationship as part of the ongoing life of the Christian community.

Another way of putting this is to say that Spirituality is to do with a relationship with God and other people. Communion is relationship; unless I am deeply committed or converted, I am not likely to want to live and love and talk with God or other people. But if I am 'facing Jesus', then all my life will be prayer. The essential prayer is that of Jesus himself, and I pray when I become part of that prayer, whatever I am doing. Spirituality is therefore becoming part of the Prayer of Jesus.

## The devotional life of the Christian community and its caring capacity

Spirituality is the whole life-style of the community as it turns to Jesus in the life of the city, or wherever it happens to be. This is why worship has to be real and relevant and alive with spontaneity, enabling people to contribute and participate, and liturgical order helping them to understand what is the length and breadth of the prayer of Jesus. I believe that spirituality is worked out in direct relation to a community, in terms of Bible reading, joining in prayers, in the communion of bread and people, in the teaching of word and discussion, and all is very near to Acts, chapter 2. More thinking and experimenting needs to be done in Christian communities to discern how this can go on being demonstrated in practice.

It is when it maintains a real spirituality of this nature that the Christian community becomes the kind of community where caring takes place. There is great support and strength to be found in such a community. There is also the opportunity for contributing the strengths and insights that we have to the thinking and worshipping and praying life of the community. We play our part at such times in caring for others and in reaching out to wholeness ourselves, which is also part of the caring or 'curing' process.

The Cure of Souls is a bringing of people together to wholeness, and the devotional, worshipping life of the Christian community plays an important role in enabling that to happen. It may be that the cure of our society and of individuals today depends very much on the discovery of a new life-style, which is what spirituality is all about.

## Questions for discussion

1. Is there a developing spirituality in your Christian community? What particular things can enable this to happen?

2. Read Acts 2:42–47. Should this be a description of a present day community?

3. Do you find your spiritual life to be aided by being alone or by sharing with other people?

4. How do you see prayer to be related to life and in particular to the caring work of the Christian community?

94